River Rocks Publishing

Front cover: Not only has the Masonic Hall been in continuous use since it was built in 1910, but it also retains most of its architectural integrity. It reminds us that historic buildings were made to last if properly taken care of.

Title page: This artwork, by Harry Moyer, was published on the front page of the *Fort William Daily Times Journal* on June 5, 1916. The banner originally said 'Welcome'; a greeting to the members of the Canadian Press Association who were in the Twin Cities for their annual meeting.

The Last Best Places

storytelling about Thunder Bay's historic buildings

Tania L. Saj

Copyright © 2009 Tania L. Saj

All rights reserved. The use of any part of this publication reproduced, transmitted in any form or by any means electronic, mechanical, photocopying, recording or otherwise, or stored in a retrieval system, without the prior written consent of the publisher—or, in the case of photocopying or other reprographic copying, a license from the Canadian Copyright Licensing Agency—is an infringement of the copyright law.

Library and Archives Canada Cataloguing in Publication
Saj, Tania L., 1971–
The Last Best Places:
storytelling about Thunder Bay's historic buildings/ Tania L. Saj

Includes bibliographical references and index.
ISBN 978-0-9782721-1-1
1. Thunder Bay (Ont.)—Buildings, structures, etc.—History. 2. Historic buildings—Social aspects—Ontario—Thunder Bay.
3. Thunder Bay (Ont.)—History I. Title

Printed and bound in Canada by Friesens
The text (pages) of this book has been printed on 100% recycled and acid-free paper

Published in Canada by River Rocks Publishing
Thunder Bay, Ontario
www.riverrocks.ca

ENVIRONMENTAL BENEFITS STATEMENT

River Rocks Publishing saved the following resources by printing the pages of this book on chlorine free paper made with 100% post-consumer waste.

TREES	WATER	SOLID WASTE	GREENHOUSE GASES
16 FULLY GROWN	7,156 GALLONS	434 POUNDS	1,486 POUNDS

Calculations based on research by Environmental Defense and the Paper Task Force.
Manufactured at Friesens Corporation

Mixed Sources
Cert no. SW-COC-001271
© 1996 FSC
FSC

For my mom,
Elle Andra-Warner

Contents

Acknowledgements

I was very fortunate to have had so many people help me with the creation of this book. First and foremost, my deepest thanks to Dawn Kannegiesser-Mitchell, my dear friend and collaborator, who was such a great support through all aspects of this project: from scouting out buildings to editing the book. It would have been a much lesser book without her input and insights. Thanks for pushing me right up until the end. I would also like to thank my mother, Elle Andra-Warner, whose heritage postcards of Thunder Bay motivated me to find out more about my hometown. And a big thank you to her for all of the leg-work she did to bring this book together.

I owe a huge debt of gratitude to Dr. Wayne O. McCready, Director of the Calgary Institute for the Humanities (CIH), Univeristy of Calgary, for helping me shape my ideas about place-making and identity. His generosity and scholarship created a wonderful work environment at CIH, where I was fortunate to have a fellowship in 2007 and where much of the research for this book was done. I would also like to thank Denise Hamel and Lorraine Ellert of CIH for the assistance and kindness they showed me during my fellowship.

This book went through many revisions thanks to the superb editorial work of Dawn Kannegiesser-Mitchell, Mark Chochla, Dr. Wayne O. McCready and Elle Andra-Warner. I truly appreciate the time they spent reading the manuscript and the constructive criticism they provided. In particular, thank you to Mark Chochla for sharing his historical acumen. Of course, any errors that may occur in the book are mine and mine alone.

So many individuals contributed to different sections of the book. Thank you to Captain David Ratz for providing information on the 96th Regiment. To Matt Szybalski, Manager and City Archivist of the Thunder Bay Archives, and Lorna Veal of the City's Planning Division, for tracking down information on the Abdou Block. Thank you to Dr. Tory Tronrud and Jeff Sumner of the Thunder Bay Museum for help in finding historical pictures and information on the buildings. Also thank you to Terry Hurtig for supplying information and pictures on the Mariaggi Hotel. Thank you to Bob Hewitson for providing hard to find documents on the Whalen Building to Dawn Kannegiesser-Mitchell who passed them on to me. I am also grateful to Bob Mills of the Thunder Bay Non-Profit Housing Corporation for calculating the remaining square footage of the Royal Edward Hotel. Reverend Randy Boyd of Trinity United Church and Reverend Deborah H. Kraft of St. Paul's Anglican Church generously allowed me access to their churches. Further thanks to Mary Richardson and Nancy Doherty who filled me in on the history of St. Paul's Anglican Church. Kathryn Dwyer of the Northwestern Ontario Sports Hall of Fame kindly supplied me with information on the Port Arthur Senior Hockey Team. Thanks to Jo-Anne Colby of CPR Archives who provided me with information on the Kaministiquia Hotel. And way back in the beginning, thank you to Kaisa Twarog for doing *something* about the Canadian Bank of Commerce.

A very big thank you to the staff at the Reference Desk at the Brodie Street Library for helping me find over a hundred local history files (a fabulous resource that provided the backbone of this book), microfilms and pictures from their collection; thank you for being so accommodating and patient with my many requests.

Sadly, I would like to posthumously thank Heather Saaltink for the work she did on the City of Thunder Bay's heritage webpages and for providing me with information from the City Clerk's files.

Thank you also to the following institutions and individuals for permission to use their images: Thunder Bay Public Library, Thunder Bay Archives, Thunder Bay Museum, Library and Archives Canada, Canada Science and Technology Museum (Ottawa), Archives of Manitoba, Toronto Public Library, Elle Andra-Warner, Dawn Kannegiesser-Mitchell, Mary Richardson, and James Kingston.

I am very grateful to the people who allowed me to interview them about their buildings. Thank you to Richard Wronowski for the many interesting discussions we had in his bakery, *European Bakery*. Thank you to Gilles Mondoux for sharing the history of his building, *Furniture Recycle*. Thank you to James Kingston for generously giving me a tour of the Masonic Hall. Thank you also to my stepfather Glenn Warner for organizing the tour. I would also like to thank Ahsanul Habib not only for allowing me to interview him several times about his buildings, but also for his passion for Thunder Bay's architecture and historic buildings. I am grateful to him for saving my favourite building in Thunder Bay, the Canadian Bank of Commerce.

I would also like to thank Jeffrey Mehagan for writing one of the most fascinating sections of the book ('Unseen Places'). I truly appreciate him taking the time to share his unique knowledge about Thunder Bay. And thank you to Elle Andra-Warner for doing a wonderful job in writing about her memories of being a schoolgirl at St. James Public School.

Once again, my deepest gratitude to Andrew Elvish for creating another beautiful cover.

Finally, I would like to thank my husband, Kevin Scott, for all of his help, all of the time. I couldn't have done it without you. And to our little son, Alexander, whose afternoon naps (aided by help from Nana and Grandma) allowed me to finally finish this book.

Introduction

There are but two strong conquerors of the forgetfulness of men,
Poetry and Architecture

John Ruskin, The Seven Lamps of Architecture

A few years ago my mother started buying postcards of Thunder Bay on *eBay*. At first, I didn't pay too much attention; I figured I had seen enough postcards of Kakabeka Falls and Old Fort William to last me for awhile.

But then I realized she wasn't buying those kinds of cards; she was buying heritage postcards of Fort William and Port Arthur (something I didn't even know existed). Pretty soon she had amassed quite a collection—but it wasn't until she showed me one of her recent additions, a postcard of Fort William's old City Hall, that I started to pay attention.

I peppered her with questions: this stunning red-brick building with its soaring tower had once graced our city? Was she sure? Had she seen it with her own eyes? I couldn't believe that such a beautiful building had once been a part of our city.

And furthermore, why in the world wasn't it still standing? I pictured the current City Hall. How could somebody think it was a good idea to tear down a beautiful brick and sandstone building and replace it with a drab, concrete box?

It seemed like a cruel joke.

City Hall, c 1910. Population of Fort William 5,000. (Collection E. Andra-Warner)

This one image gave me a completely different vision of my hometown. I was determined to find out more. I wondered about all of the other buildings that had been torn down before my time and about all of the parking lots and vacant fields I had seen 'go up' in recent years.

What other secrets were out there?

City Hall, 2007. The building underwent significant renovations in 2009. (Photo Tania L. Saj)

I also began to wonder about the *consequences* of tearing down historic buildings. Did it matter to the citizens of Thunder Bay that some of their landmark buildings were missing? Was 'progress' always a good excuse for demolition? What about the social and cultural ties that people have to the built environment? What happens to those ties when familiar places are gone?

But I wasn't done there, I had more questions. Wasn't it *wasteful* to tear down these buildings? What about all of the *embodied energy* stored up in old buildings—the non-recoverable energy that goes into manufacturing and transporting the building supplies required to build the building; as well as the resources required to construct the building? For example, a typical building built in the mid–20th century required the equivalent of 5 to 15 gallons of gas per square foot to construct. It is pretty much wasted if that building is torn down. If we are diligent about recycling our pop cans and milk containers, why don't we recycle old buildings? Is it because old buildings are inherently energy inefficient? Was an old building always going to lose out when compared to a new building? If so, I might as well write this book as an eulogy rather than a celebration of history. And I had better hurry, as some of my favourite buildings were currently facing the wrecking ball.

These questions steered my research and I found the book taking shape in three different directions.

My first goal is to (re)acquaint people with the history and stories of Thunder Bay's historic buildings. As I found out, these buildings can tell some pretty good tales—like the one about the fortune teller who read palms on Hardisty Street or the midnight balls at the Mariaggi Hotel (or the bear that lived in the basement). Finding these stories has made all of the difference to me, and the Thunder Bay I thought I knew at the start of the book—a bland child of the 1970 amalgamation, and the Thunder Bay I knew at the end—a vibrant and historically-rooted elder, were two completely different cities.

Second, this book is care for the soul. We have lost so many great buildings in Thunder Bay, in such a short period of time. This book is for all of the people who feel a twinge of sadness at the sight of a wrecking ball; yet, we try to convince ourselves, progress is progress; a box store in the Intercity area is a more convenient way to do our shopping. But this book suggests we do have a right to our sadness. Historic buildings *root* us and help us care about our environment. A prerequisite for a healthy community.

And third, I had to find out if it made economic and/or environmental sense to keep historic buildings. I could already hear my skeptics—it was well and good to appreciate historic buildings, but they were economic/energetic dinosaurs. In the energy conscious world we live in, where 'green-building' design and LEED (Leadership in Energy and Environmental Design) certification gives you bragging rights—how much do historic buildings contribute to sustainable development? Quite a lot actually. As I will discuss, the preservation/ reuse of historic buildings and sustainable development are natural allies.

A note on reading this book: start anywhere. This book does not have to be read in order. When writing this book, I thought of each building as its own character, and let the buildings speak for themselves, which sometimes entailed telling their stories through newspaper articles, interviews, pictures or narrative.

Flip to a building that strikes your fancy and read about that one, perhaps you might even want to grab a cup of coffee and take a drive–by after you are done. Or you may have more stories that need telling; in which case, call up your children or grandchildren and tell them about the time you danced the night away at the Royal Eddie or took your first swimming lesson in the scratchy pool at the YMCA.

Thunder Bay, we need to tell our stories. I hope this book becomes as much of an interactive experience for you as it was for me.

Place-Making

Sense of place rests its case on the unexamined premise that being from somewhere is always preferable to being from nowhere.

Keith H. Basso, Wisdom Sits in Places

During the research process, I was fortunate to come across a book called *Wisdom Sits in Places* by Keith H. Basso. It is a book about 'place–making', a term I had never heard of before, but it quickly shaped my thoughts on writing this book.

Basso explains that place–making is a universal tool of remembering and imagining: "What people make of their places is closely connected to what they make of themselves." In essence, if you have ever wondered: "What happened here? Who was involved? What was it like? Why should it matter?" you are place-making.

In *Wisdom Sits in Places,* Basso describes how the Apache people cultivate a relationship between storytelling and the physical landscape. Storytelling is an important means of getting a message across in order to reinforce moral directives and societal norms in this culture. Writes Basso: "Stories go to work on your mind and make you think about your life…After stories and storytellers have served this beneficial purpose, features of the physical landscape take over and perpetuate it. Mountains and arroyos step in symbolically for grandmothers and uncles."

For example, you can gather the meaning of a steep slope in Apache country called *She Carries Her Brother On Her Back.* I began to see Thunder Bay's 'built environment' in a similar light.

I began to think of all of the stories our buildings could tell: "What happened here?" was constantly running through my head. And then I started to realize that many of Thunder Bay's historic buildings were also meaning–laden.

Basso's book helped me formulate the main thesis of this book: that storytelling is necessary for place–making which is necessary to being rooted—I'll explain why being rooted is important later—and that physical locations, whether built or natural, are the devices that anchor storytelling.

Here are a couple of examples of how we can do place–making in Thunder Bay. Let's take the example of the Young Men's Christian Association (YMCA), the building formerly at the corner of Miles and Archibald; if you do not know the building's history, its rich connection to the city is lost. But once you have learned the inspiring story about how the YMCA was built, it is easy to understand why I nick–named it: *The Building That Looks Ahead: What Is A Child Worth?* (Although the current fashion is to shorten names to their smallest possible permutation, an acronym is preferable, I feel there is nothing wrong with a descriptive name that gives it to you straight and tells you what you need to know.)

The same goes for the Royal Edward Hotel on May Street. Once you know its history, you realize its other name is: *The Hotel That Community Pride Built And Then Forgot.*

And with all of the comings and goings at the CNR station at the Marina, you will understand why I nick–named it: *The Place Of Joy And Sadness.*

Place–making can help us turn undifferentiated 'spaces', localities without strong meaning or value, into humanized 'places' of value (Tuan, 1977). Think of all of the stories you could tell about places in Thunder Bay. Let's call these stories your *I–Place* relationships. You have been creating these relationships, mostly unconsciously, since childhood. Ian Nairn writes:

> It seems commonplace that almost everyone is born with the need for identification with his surroundings and a relationship to them—with the need to be in a recognizable place. So sense of place is not a fine art extra, it is something we cannot afford to do without.

But chances are your stories of places do not only involve yourself. They involve other people. Place–making reinforces our interrelationships with each other: we share stories about "What happened here? Who was involved? What was it like? Why should it matter?"

Our *collected* memories of a place (not *collective*, because our memories can be different, good and bad simultaneously) create a link between ourselves and the community: think of these relationships as *I–We–Place* relationships.

Our *I–Place* and *I–We–Place* relationships shape us and are shaped by us. Edward Relph in *Place and Placelessness* writes:

> A deep relationship with places is as necessary, and perhaps as unavoidable, as close relationships with people; without such relationships human existence, while possible, is bereft of much of its significance.

Simply put, we need these relationships to be fully human. I firmly believe that storytelling is the way home; back to a sense of the city and, more importantly, a sense of ourselves.

The buildings in the following section are all well–known buildings that I felt needed to have their 'forgotten' stories told. Stories that had slipped through the cracks or were patchily known by the average person. Although many other stories could be told about these buildings, I chose the stories that jumped out at me and seemed to capture the special spirit of the building.

Learning about these stories also confirmed that place–making works. Without realizing it, these stories had a transformative effect on me. The more I read and learned, the more I felt an almost sticky, web–like connection being made between myself and the city, 'spaces' were turning into 'places'. My truncated, shallower relationship with Thunder Bay was transforming into a much more meaningful one.

CNR Station

Canadian National Railway Station at the Marina, c 1910 (Collection EAW)

Year Built: 1906
Architect: Ralph B. Bratt
Style: Railway Gothic
Heritage Status: City of Thunder Bay Heritage Property

The Marina is a special place in Thunder Bay. Not only is the view of Lake Superior and the Sleeping Giant spectacular, it is also a place of local and national historical significance.

Originally called The Depot, The Landing or The Station, Port Arthur can trace its roots to these very shores. It all started in 1870, when Colonel Wolseley and his troops set up their headquarters at the site of the present–day Marina. The Colonel was on his way to the Red River to quell Louis Riel's Rebellion. The Depot was their stopping–off point before making the back–breaking trek over Northwestern Ontario's unforgiving terrain, which sometimes required the men to *pull* their boats through the swampy forest.

The Colonel found a fledgling community here in 1870, as described by one of his soldiers, Captain Scott, in a letter home:

There was a small village at The Landing, composed of two small stores, a tavern called Hotel de Flaherty, two or three private residences and a large number of government buildings, stables, sheds, etc., etc.

Colonel Wolseley's camp, Prince Arthur's Landing, 1870 (National Archives)

A letter from Hugh John MacDonald (1850-1929), a member of Wolseley's Red River Expedition and the son of Canada's first Prime Minister Sir John A. MacDonald, to a friend about the challenging travel conditions in Northwestern Ontario.

Oskondaga Creek, Dawson's Road, July 15, 1870

Things went on very quietly at Thunder Bay from the date of my last letter till Monday the 4th at three o'clock in the morning when we were all up, and ready to start on the march up the road. At about four o'clock the start was effected, the delay being caused by a good many of the men and some of the officers being drunk as the devil. Of course this is private and confidential as I would not like to have circulated. However, at last we got off and that day marched 13 miles, part of the time through a heavy thunderstorm....

Next morning we were up and off at two o'clock and marched as far as the Kamanistiquia Bridge where we halted, and camped and were just preparing to make ourselves comfortable, when Col. Wolseley rode into camp and ordered our Coy. and No. 7 to continue to march next day. In accordance with these orders, at four the next morning we began a long march of twenty-five miles, over terribly muddy roads in which you would sink up to your ankles every step. The worst of it was that the soil is damned stiff red clay and sticks to one's feet like the devil. A good many men gave out on the road and came straggling into camp some time after we arrived....We then pitched our tents, had supper and went to bed, having first heartily cursed old Dawson. He may perhaps call this a "good road" but in any civilized country it would pass for a very respectable swamp. We are encamped about a mile from Oskondaga Creek, a place abounding with mosquitos, black flies, sand flies, and other game. None of them trouble me, thank God, but all go for the Captain. I really believe that the devil got up this expedition for the purpose of getting hold of my immortal soul, as I am already beginning to swear a little. The example set me by my Captain is not good, as I am sorry to say he does not bear the bites of the mosquito, doubtless made by the Lord, with the patience of a Christian, and whenever evening approaches my ears are shocked by oaths.

Although Wolseley didn't get his man (Riel had fled over the U.S. border before his soldiers arrived), the expedition did put Prince Arthur's Landing on the map. Politicians and homesteaders in the east took notice of this quiet, frontier town. Although it required grueling, fly–bitten labour to make the overland journey from the head of Lake Superior to the Red River, Wolseley proved that it *could* be done.

Boom years followed. Westbound traffic increased and the silver rush of the 1870s brought an influx of miners, speculators and merchants to the Landing.

But biggest of all was the railway. On July 8, 1882, after a 30–hour journey from Winnipeg, the first train arrived at Prince Arthur's Landing. The *Port Arthur Weekly Herald* captured the celebrations:

Yesterday morning the news was received here that a through train was on its way and would arrive here late at night. The news was spread like wildfire, and it was not long before everyone in town knew it.

About midnight a bonfire was started on the esplanade in front of the Queen's Hotel [Author Note: site of the future Mariaggi Hotel] and soon a crowd gathered around, waiting anxiously for the long-expected visitor. At last, shortly before one o'clock, the sound of the whistle was heard and the headlight of the engine was seen in the distance. As the train neared the Queen's Hotel, guns were fired off, and cheer after cheer filled the air.

The railway changed everything. From that point on, thousands of immigrants passed through the Twin Cities on their way west. In 1911, a Port Arthur newspaper reported 26 westbound trains passed through the city in a 48–hour period. The future of the two cities was assured.

The CNR Station is in the background, c 1910 (Collection EAW)

The importance of the railway to the growth of Thunder Bay cannot be overstated; and one of the best reminders of this legacy is the Canadian National Railway Station at the Marina.

Built in 1906, the station is a beautiful example of 'Railway Gothic' architecture, a distinctly Canadian style of architecture designed by the CPR and CNR for their train stations and hotels (picture the Banff Springs Hotel). It is a grandiose style of architecture that invokes the look of a European castle or chateau. The Marina station is the only example of Railway Gothic architecture in the city, a work of art really, rather than a building, with its canvas of dark–red Wisconsin brick and Tyndall, Manitoba limestone, accented by medieval–looking turrets and stone reliefs. Although its interior has undergone significant renovations over the past 100 years, we can still take a peak inside *circa* 1906 thanks to an article published in the *Fort William Daily Times News* detailing its decor:

On the ground floor are located general and ladies' waiting rooms, baggage room and ticket office. The ladies' waiting room is at the north end of the building, and the

ticket office between it and the general waiting room. Modernly equipped lavatories are provided for each waiting room. At the south end of the station is the baggage room. A feature which will commend itself to travellers, especially during the boating and tourist season, is the provision of a parcel room where parcels, valises, coats, etc., many be checked for a nominal charge....The whole building, with the exception of the agent's living rooms, is finished with a burlap wainscoting, which has a very serviceable as well as artistic appearance. The interior woodwork, doors, window sashes, etc., of the main floor are of oak and the floors of maple. The waiting rooms are lighted by globular incandescent lamps of ground glass in clusters of four, with oxydized copper fixtures.

The woodwork on the second floor is of Georgian pine, and on this floor are the offices of Superintendent Cameron, the Superintendent's chief clerk, the dispatchers, resident engineer, roadmaster, bridge and building inspector, customs officer, and also the private office of the agent, Mr. Phalen.

The general freight offices are located at the north end of the building on the third floor and the remainder of the floor is occupied by the living apartments provided for the agent, Mr. Phalen, whose quarters consist of four rooms, including a large bathroom, on this floor, and three rooms and a hall on the second floor, all at the south end of the building.

Despite the station's noble history, and the many thousands of people who had passed through its doors, by the 1970s traffic was down and the station closed; the city took it over in 1977. For years, the station's future was uncertain and it faced numerous threats to demolish it, but in the end, it survived and was finally incorporated into the city's waterfront plans.

So many waves of humanity have passed by this spot, so many comings and goings, so many conflicting emotions, I found it difficult to select which stories should represent this important building. But I finally narrowed it down to two stories that I felt spoke to the joy and sadness that this building has seen.

The first is a little known story about Thunder Bay's brush with the Stanley Cup. Yes, *the* Stanley Cup. In 1911, the Port Arthur Senior Hockey Team played the Ottawa Senators for the most coveted trophy in hockey. Yes, *the* Ottawa Senators. The 'Port Arthurs', as the local newspapers called them, were the National Hockey Association Western Champions, which gave them the right to play the Eastern Champions in the Stanley Cup finals. In the following article, we meet the Port Arthurs at the train station where they have just arrived from Winnipeg. Even though the train is nine hours late, thousands of people are waiting to congratulate them. After an impromptu celebration, the boys are off again to Ottawa.

In Times of Joy: Playing for the Stanley Cup

Port Arthur Daily News, March 13, 1911

THOUSANDS OUT TO GREET RETURNING HOCKEY TEAM

Players Received by Probably the Biggest Crowd That Ever Gathered on Port Arthur Streets—Speeches and Supper at Lyceum

When the Port Arthur hockey team arrived home last evening from Winnipeg, where it won the

championship of Western Canada and qualified for the right to represent this part of the Dominion in a game for the Stanley Cup, it was met at the Canadian Northern Station by a crowd that numbered anywhere from two to four thousand people. It seemed as if almost the whole city had turned out to welcome the victorious hockey players for not only was the whole station platform crowded but people were massed along the opposite side of Water Street and in the lower parts of Park, Lorne, and Arthur [Red River Road] Streets, in crowds that could not be estimated. The train was about nine hours late, arriving at 9:15, instead of noon.

Immense Crowd

The crowds began to gather early in the evening and were in full strength some time before the train arrived. The band was out and played a number of airs while the people were waiting. When the train's headlight was seen coming from the west a cheer ran through the crowd, and the band played again. The train came slowly into the station through an avenue lined with humanity.

Along the platform supporters of the team had drawn green and white ribbons, and as the train came to a standstill, and the players and rooters who had gone with them to Winnipeg, disembarked, the band played 'Hail, Hail, the Gang's All Here.'

Greet the Players

As the players were seen emerging from the car, each was greeted with a cheer and with much handshaking the crowd surged with them along Arthur Street [Red River Road].

Here the ribbon carriers drew up in line and putting the players between, escorted them through the crowds to the Lyceum theatre. Manager Taney met the popular desire when he threw open the doors of the theatre, though those who did get inside formed but a small portion of the crowds that had gathered about the streets. The proceedings inside the theatre were brief and to the point. Mayor Ray presided, but no aldermen were in evidence, and none of the other city officials took the platform.

Lyceum Theatre, Cumberland Street, 2007 (Photo TLS)

In fact the only two speakers of the evening were the Mayor and Captain McDonough. The remarks made by these gentlemen, however, gave the crowd in the theatre plenty of opportunity to cheer and show in a vociferous way their appreciation of the deeds of valour done by the players. On appearing on the platform Mayor Ray was received with applause. He said:

The Mayor's Speech

"I feel exceedingly proud to be Mayor of this city, to welcome you back. We are proud of your performance in the Stanley Cup test games and your success as hockeyists and the victory is doubly appreciated because we have not heard one word against the manner in which you have won the victory.

"Every citizen of this town knows that you have accomplished something that brings credit and honour to the city. You can see that the citizens have appreciated your victory in turning out in thousands this evening. It has been the custom, as far as I know and have read from history, for successful warriors, and those who have gained triumphs of every sort, to receive high commendation at the hands of their fellow citizens when they return with laurels placed upon their brows, and we are here carrying out that custom.

"I am pleased," continued the Colonel, "as are the rest of us, to have you here this evening although it is Sunday, but had it been any other evening we would have given you a demonstration that would have lived long in the minds of yourselves and of all those who would have seen it and participated in it, and it would have been because we all appreciated what you have done.

"Sometimes young men go from home and win by unfair methods, and yet get credit for their victories, but you have won fairly and brought credit and honour to Port Arthur and its hockey club. Your antagonists were no mean men by any means, but good, strong hockey players. Had you had to have gone up against poor men we would not have esteemed you so much, but against men worthy of your steel it is all the more honour and you have shown that we have steel worthy of them in Port Arthur."

Known Everywhere

The Mayor then alluded to the fact that all over Canada and the northern part of the United States where hockey was played, the name of the hockey team of Port Arthur was on the lips of hundreds of thousands.

"Therefore, it is right that this city should show appreciation of the honour brought here," commented the Mayor.

"Yesterday afternoon prominent citizens thought the victory deserved some recognition from the council as representing the ratepayers, and after discussing the form it should take, the council have decided to offer the boys the sum of $500 to help defray their expenses in going to Ottawa to win further laurels."

This announcement was received with great cheering and on resuming His Worship said that some of the council thought the public would not be in favour of the proposal but if the public were not in favour of it for such a cause, well— — —, and the Mayor made a most expressive gesture.

He was satisfied that all the well-meaning citizens with manliness in their hearts had a great regard for the manliness of that team of theirs.

He remarked that they would have a hard row to hoe, and a voice yelled: "They will win."

The Colonel said he hoped so, and whether they won or lost when they returned, they would be received in a fitting manner.

"You will have to face many difficulties," concluded the Mayor, addressing himself more particularly to the players, "such as soft ice, a long journey, and face people who are strange. I hope for your victory, but if you are defeated, I know you will come home with honour, and as long as you play a square, honest game, we will stand behind you in this city of Port Arthur.

"Gentlemen, I can only give you the city of Port Arthur, and you can have it."

Paddy's Speech

The Mayor was loudly cheered and he called on Captain McDonough, who was, he hoped, as good an orator as he was hockeyist.

Three cheers having been given for the team, Captain McDonough expressed the honour that he felt, but would not say much, as they had to catch the next train for the east.

They hoped to go to Ottawa and make as good a showing as they did in the west. They did not expect such a reception last night but, "Believe me," he said, "if we go to Ottawa and win this cup, we shall rather expect a little reception—if we don't we shan't be looking for it," a conclusion that was heartily cheered.

At the conclusion of Paddy McDonough's speech, Mayor Ray called upon any other members of the team who wished to say anything in regard to the trip. No reply was received and he closed the meeting with a wave of his hand and, "The meeting is adjourned, gentlemen."

The members of the team and many of their admirers then repaired to the Lyceum grill where a sumptuous dinner was waiting.

Port Arthur Daily News, March 13, 1911

PORT ARTHURS GO TO OTTAWA TO PLAY GAME FOR THE STANLEY CUP

Left for East Two Hours After Arrival From West—Play Sudden Death Game Thursday—Meikle Goes Along

Two hours after arriving in Port Arthur on their return from their victorious trip to Winnipeg, where they went for the championship of the west, the Port Arthur hockey team was on its way to Ottawa in search of the Stanley Cup.

The same team will represent the Port Arthurs at Canada's capital as at the western metropolis with the exception that Meikle went along in place of Ward. Meikle having been prevented from going to Winnipeg by injuries received in the last game with the Thunder Bays.

— — — —

There is no doubt about Meikle being a source of strength to the team as he is as good a hockeyist as ever produced in Port Arthur and one whom every Port Arthur citizen would be delighted to see on the team representing the city. At the same time the management of the team dislikes to leave O'Leary off, after having gone through the league season with the team and having done pretty good work.

This is especially so in view of the fact that going to Ottawa he is going to his hometown where he is well-known and where many will want to see him in action. According to a statement made to *The Daily News* by one of the Port Arthur club's executive last evening, O'Leary and Meikle will probably both be played in the Stanley Cup game. This contest will be in three twenty-minute periods and teams have the option of changing players up to the commencement of the third period.

— — — —

The train bearing the players is due to arrive in Ottawa tomorrow morning at 5 o'clock and this will give the players a chance for a couple of workouts on the Ottawa ice so that they should become fairly familiar with the size and shape of the rink. They will also have an opportunity of visiting the Parliament buildings and other sites.

— — — —

But with all this talk about the game at Ottawa there is today a slight uncertainty about it taking place. It must be remembered that tonight the Galt team, champions of the Ontario pro league, play the Ottawas [The Senators] in a sudden death game for the cup. It is generally expected that Ottawa will win, but Galt has a husky, speedy and experienced aggregation and might spring a surprise. In such a case, Port Arthur would have to go on to Galt to play.

— — — —

Before leaving for Ottawa, Captain McDonough of the Port Arthur team said to *The Daily News*: "I haven't had very much experience in giving

interviews to newspapers, but you can say that the boys are going to Ottawa with just the same feeling that we went to Winnipeg, that is determined to play the best game we have in us.

"I know the Ottawas are the fastest team in Canada and have a great advantage in the matter of experience and the fact that they will be playing on their own ice before a home crowd. But if we get hard ice we are not at all afraid of what we can do.

"We believe we are just as speedy as the big league champions. I am not going to say we are going to win and I am not going to say we will lose. The only thing I can say—we will do our best and hope that best will be good enough to satisfy the people of Port Arthur."

This story, of course, would be much better known had the Port Arthurs won. However, it was the Ottawa Senators who won the Cup by a score of 13 to 4. The headline read: "Port Arthurs Play a Fast Game But Are Beaten By Inside Hockey". Despite the lopsided score, apparently they put up a good fight. A local reporter filed this report from Ottawa: "Although the score at the finish of sixty minutes of play was 13 to 4 in favour of the National Hockey Association champions this hardly represents the play. As for actual mid-ice hockey, in skating and stickhandling, the men who came down from the west appeared to be in every way as good as the local seven."

Now for our second story. Five years after the Port Arthurs played for the Stanley Cup, the station was the scene of a more sombre departure. On June 9, 1916, 1,385 boys of the 94th New Ontario Battalion, a battalion made up of local boys from

Northwestern Ontario, shipped out to Valcartier, Quebec before sailing on to join World War I. Despite its small population, Northwestern Ontario managed to send three battalions to the Great War—the 52nd, 94th and 141st.

On that June day, thousands of people lined Red River Road, Cumberland Street and Water Street, waving flags and thrusting parcels filled with home–baked goods into the hands of the passing soldiers. It was a sad, but proud day, as the soldiers lined up on the platform to say goodbye to their family and friends; perhaps none more poignant than the goodbyes between Louis Northan and his nine children, or the mother who said goodbye to her third son. For 205 boys of the 94th, these were their last goodbyes. Lest we forget.

In Times of Sadness: World War I

Fort William Daily Times Journal, June 9, 1916

TOUCHING SCENES WHEN 94TH ENTRAINED TODAY

Citizens of Two Communities Turn Out En Masse To Give Boys Send-Off

At Port Arthur

With tear-dimmed eyes yet with many a hearty cheer the citizens of Fort William and Port Arthur this morning bade farewell to the boys of the 94th battalion who left for their summer camp. The first train, a special of 14 cars which conveyed the boys from the steel plant, West Fort William passed through Port Arthur shortly after nine o'clock and the crowds of

people gathered at the depot and in the vicinity cheered the brave boys.

Long before the hour of departure the Canadian Northern platform, north and south Water Street, the Canadian Pacific railway station square and east Arthur Street [Red River Road] were crowded with solid blocks of people eager to say goodbye to the boys. It is estimated that even at the early hour of eight o'clock there were over 3,000 people out to see the last of the soldiers. Nearly everybody carried a parcel. In many instances more than one, and homemade cooking, candy, fruit, cigars, cigarettes, chewing gum, papers and magazines were pressed into the hands of the soldiers.

Recruitment ad for the 94th Battalion *Fort William Daily Times Journal*, 1916.

The Port Arthur Boys

At eight o'clock the Port Arthur detachment of the 94th left the Armouries and the lifting strains of music of the fine brass band could be heard as they led the companies down the street. The contingent headed by Col. Machin, made a gallant showing. The men were all carrying full service equipment, weighing 73 pounds, but so evenly distributed that the weight was not burdensome. All were merry and bright.

As soon as the men were drawn up on Water Street and ordered to 'stand at ease', it was with difficulty that the ranks were kept, so eager were relatives and friends to have the last word and handshake. At nine-thirty, the long special train came in, and the boys were speedily entrained. All the local boys in the 94th are very well-known in the Twin Cities, so are the officers. In many cases they have mobilized here from other points and have made friends, so that every soldier had friends in the crowd, and everybody on the crowd knew one or more—generally more—of the soldiers.

Popular Officers

Colonel Machin came in for a great ovation as he stepped aboard the train, so did Canon Hedley and Captain W.T. Denison, Lieutenants Shelly and Griffiths and others. It is not so long ago since our hearts were saddened by the departure of another well-known local battalion, but never have such scopes been enacted in Port Arthur as were witnessed today when the gallant boys of the 94th left for their summer camp, shortly to go overseas.

Pathetic Farewells

Pathetic scenes were witnessed. One very prominent young businessman of Port Arthur, his eyes filled with tears, stated to the *Times Journal* that he was overwhelmed with sympathetic sorrow at the sorrowing leave takings that were being enacted on the platform.

Louis Northan, 153 Pine Street, Port Arthur, was the centre of a very pathetic little home group. Round him were gathered his wife and nine children ranging from a little babe in arms to grown up daughters. None made any attempt to conceal their emotion, except the father, who was the bravest of them all, and 'kept a stiff upper lip'.

All along the line were pathetic scenes. Girls who had known some of the boys from their childhood were there to say and kiss them good-bye. Everyone in town knew one or more of the boys, and by the time ten o'clock had arrived and the long special was still in the vicinity of the station, packing the platform to suffocation, crowding and completely blocking the streets, filling the verandas of the Mariaggi, the windows, and office spaces of the freight office, the publicity Pagoda steps and even the Canadian Pacific Railway platform.

So dense was the crowd that it extended up Arthur Street [Red River Road] to Cumberland. But it was an orderly crowd. The people had all to an individual only one object in view—to say goodbye to the boys.

Three Boys From One Family

When the last well-known battalion went away from the head of the lakes, it will be remembered that coming down the street to the station was a young Port Arthur man with a basket full of good things for his brother who went away with the battalion, 'pasties for Tom', he shouted out with glee, and today that same brother and yet another brother went with the 94th making three brave brothers in all from one family.

The parents and sisters were down at the train this morning to see the brothers off and bore up bravely when the time for parting came. The brothers were not forgotten, though, by many friends and three luscious fresh pastries found their way into the boys' bundles.

Just before leaving a message was flashed down the cars that the Austrians were reported by bulletin this morning to have lost 200,000 men in the last few days. This was greeted with cheers, and one brawny soldier shouted out, 'Never mind that; it's the Kaiser we're after."

The Fort William Men

The Fort William contingent arrived at Port Arthur at 9:20 am, and stayed nine minutes to allow some heavy baggage being loaded. As they pulled to the cheers of the assembled populace, the 94th band played 'Auld

Lange Syne' and 'God Save the King'. Then came the long line of empties for the Port Arthur boys.

Sentries were posted at each door and the men entrained in a wonderfully orderly manner winding their way through the crowds without any pushing aside of women or children, in spite of the heavy equipment they were carrying. It was 10:15 am when the special left the Port Arthur depot. Slowly, apparently almost with reluctance, and the crowd was just as loath to let the boys go. But they have gone, and they have left behind them memories of dutiful sons, loving husbands and affectionate fathers, and the prayers of thousands of anxious relatives and friends will go up that they may have a safe and victorious return.

The Port Arthur City Band, which had played this morning at the station in Fort William, having been on duty with the band since 7 o'clock, played the train out of the station to the strains of 'God Save the King'. The familiar music of 'Auld Lange Syne' warned the crowd that the time for departure was at hand.

Cheer upon cheer rent the air as familiar faces were seen at the car windows. On the front of the caboose, alone, stood the Chaplain, Reverend Canon Hedley, for 11 years rector at St. John's [Anglican] Church and a roar of cheering broke out as his solitary figure was drawn up at the salute.

Union Station

Union Station, now the Canadian Pacific Railway Station, Syndicate Avenue, c 1911 (Collection TLS)

Year Built: 1911
Architect: R.E. Mason
Style: Beaux-Arts
Heritage Status: Heritage Railway Station (Historic Sites and Monuments Board of Canada)

Not long ago, my friend Dawn Kannegiesser-Mitchell and I were having lunch at Cronos Cafe on Syndicate Avenue. From our booth, we had a wonderful view of the Canadian Pacific Railway Station across the street. After a tasty lunch of chicken souvlaki and Greek salad, we decided to take a closer look. Something seemed different about the station; but we couldn't place what. Then we realized what it was—the station looked in *better* shape that the last time we had seen it. The bricks looked redder and the stonework whiter.

Indeed, this classic Beaux-Arts train station has had a facelift. Michael Oliphant, the CPR's Service Area Manager, explained in an interview with the Thunder Bay *Chronicle Journal* (August 20, 2007) that the CPR had undertaken major renovations to restore the station. As part of the renovations, every brick of the front facade was hand–cleaned, concrete mouldings were repaired, windows were replaced with replicas of the originals, and the lamps flanking the front doors were replaced with historically accurate globe lamps. As to the cost, all Oliphant would say was that the project was "expensive".

The restoration work makes it hard to tell the 1911 station on page 34 from the 2007 station on page 38. The station seems to have hardly aged in almost 100 years.

In selecting the stories to accompany this building, I wanted to complement the CPR's restoration efforts. Therefore, I selected two stories that take us back to the opening day of the station in 1911. The opening of a railway station was no small affair, for most communities this was a political, economic and civic milestone, and they celebtrated its arrival with much pomp and ceremony. The opening of Union Station was no exception.

In the first story, we are taken on a tour of the building by the local Boy Scouts and then served tea in the rotunda at the ribbon-cutting ceremony. The reporter does a wonderful job describing the architecture—and the social customs of the time. The second article requires formal wear, as we attend the glamorous ball held that night in the station in aid of the McKellar [General] Hospital.

Fort William Daily Times Journal, April 18, 1911

ONE OF CANADA'S MOST MODERN RAILWAY STATIONS IS OPENED HERE

Women of District Entertain Large Number of Citizens in Handsome Structure Just Completed

In suitable keeping with the traditions of the C.P.R.—projecting great enterprises and performing vast undertakings without a great display of fuss the opening of the Union Station on Syndicate Avenue was performed this afternoon by the simple act of Superintendent Armstrong in charge of this division of the C.P.R. handing his key of the front entrance to the care of Mrs. F.C. Perry, president of the Local Council of Women.

Opening Delayed

The time for opening had been fixed for 3 o'clock, but a misunderstanding delayed the ceremony. The ladies meanwhile gathered in force, and while waiting were shown round the building by a detachment of Boy Scouts under F. Jones. The main vestibule was packed with chairs to accommodate the visitors, and from the room which will in future be devoted to the melling of papers and regard. The ladies connected with the local council made preparations for and dispensed afternoon tea.

Architectural drawing of Union Station, 1909. *Fort William Daily Times Journal*

Magnificent Structure

A word or two as to the building itself. The buildings over all are 280 feet by 50 feet, the height to the cornice being 55 feet from the ground.

There is a vast basement running the length of the building which really makes the working space another ten feet in height. The structure is composed of milton-faced bricks, relieved drawings and facings of Bedford stone, and though not of great architectural beauty presents a business-like and rather imposing appearance.

The idea has been to have such accommodation that should the demand of the future call for further additions these can easily be effected.

The main vestibule, in which the ceremony of the opening was held today, is finished in green oak and bases of marble, three columns supporting a lofty roof, the columns having a pedestal of marble also.

The vestibule is flanked by the newsstand and the ticket and telegram offices, with the retiring rooms beyond, while on the platform side are the usual offices pertaining to the working of the line.

All the ground floors are Italian terrazzo and the building is reinforced concrete and fireproof throughout.

The two floors of rooms above are admirably adapted for offices, and it is understood that the rooms on both floors will be divided between the C.P.R. and the G.T.P. [Grand Trunk Pacific Railway].

The restored Union Station, 2007 (Photo TLS)

As Seen By A Woman

Pride and delight in the new Fort William Union Station is manifest in the beaming faces of the throngs of guests at the reception held in the big rotunda this afternoon. Promptly at three o'clock the opening ceremonies began with addresses from the C.P.R. and G.T.P. officials, Mayor Young, Mayor Ray of Port Arthur, Dr. T.S.T. Smellie, M.P.P. and a number of others. Mrs. F.C. Perry, as president of the Local Council of Women and representing the women of the district gave a short address, in which she expressed the appreciation of the Women's Council of the act of the railway officials in placing a matron at the station to befriend the women who are travelling through here.

When the program of addresses came to an end, Superintendent R. Armstrong, with fitting ceremony presented the keys of the new building to Mrs. J.L. Tidmus, president of the Hospital Aid, and J.H. Perry, chairman of the Hospital Board, thanked the officials on their behalf. This brought the opening ceremony to a close and all formality ended, the guests wandered about the splendid building, inspecting and examining, ending up in the rotunda again where the delicious refreshments were served by the doctors' wives of the city.

The rotunda or general waiting room is bright and spacious, an ideal place for a gathering such as was held there this afternoon.

A large table centred with flowers and heaped with good things occupied one end of the room, close by the newsstand, behind which was concealed the electric heaters where the tea was brewing and kept hot.

The room is finished in oak, with marble base and granite floor. At one end is the large ticket office, and opposite it at the other end is the newsstand. On the right hand side of the main entrance is the ladies waiting room, which will be used as a dressing room this evening. It is finished in oak, with dark red burlap and is connected with one or two smaller waiting rooms and lavatories.

On the left hand side is the men's waiting room, also nicely furnished in oak with dark red burlap.

Other spacious apartments on the ground floor are the Dominion express rooms, at one end and baggage and storage rooms at the other.

Large doors facing the east lead out to a wide station platform where the reception committee will gather this evening to welcome the Port Arthur guests when their trains pull in.

A wide and handsome stairway with slate steps leads to the floors above, the first floor being devoted to offices and store rooms, the second also devoted to offices, engineers' apartments and the telegraph operators' room. The latter is a bright room at the end of the hall, and in this the ball will be held this evening. The second and third floors are finished in pine.

Fort William Daily Times Jorunal, April 18, 1911

BRILLIANT GATHERING

District Ladies Hold Ball in the New Union Station

Fort William women scored another splendid triumph in the successful carrying out of the brilliant ceremonies attendant upon the opening of the new railway station, and the city surely owes its women workers a debt of gratitude.

To the members of the Hospital Aid, under the direction of their president, Mrs. J. L. Tidmus, belong the credit and to their treasury comes the returns of yesterday's events, but women workers from every church and every charitable organization were represented among the women yesterday and brought their quota of labour to the general success.

As Superintendent Armstrong remarked yesterday, the women offered the solution to what had seemed to the railway officials to be a difficult problem, that of a fitting and appropriate opening of the new building, and all are well satisfied with the result of their decision to place the matter completely in the hands of the members of McKellar Hospital Aid, while Fort William women have added more glory and honour to the reputation already earned in the matter of planning and successfully carrying out big events of social and philanthropic importance.

More delightful and more enjoyable even than the afternoon ceremonies in the station, was the grand ball of last evening which brought ceremonies to a close.

The committee in charge was composed of Mrs. J.L. Tidmus, Mrs. Peter McKellar, Mrs. Geo. MacEdward, Mrs. James Murphy and Mrs. W.F. Hogarth, the present officers of the Hospital Aid; Mrs. G.A. Graham, Mrs. C.W. Jarvis, Mrs. D. M. Mitchell, Mrs.

T. M. Piper and Mr. N.N. Betts, past presidents: Mrs. L.L Pelltier, Mrs. J.H. Perry and Mrs. G.S. Coslett, representing the hospital board, and Mrs. J.M. Sherk and Miss Sadie Stewart, representing the press.

The large building was aglow with light from basement to roof, two orchestras—one on the first floor where the guests were received and welcomed, the other in the ballroom on the third floor—provided delightful music, while quantities of flowers used in decoration and in beautifying the large tables where the feast was spread added beauty to the scene. The throngs in attendance were even larger than had been anticipated and not the least interesting feature of the event was the number of exquisite and beautiful gowns worn by the ladies.

Among the younger set simple, becoming gowns of white, Alice blue and Helen pink were noted, but the matrons of the city never appeared to better advantage than in the fashionable and artistic gowns of satin, silk, chiffon, lace, embroidered net, and other favourite materials of the season.

Well-known men from the professional and business life of the city were present in large numbers and for those who were not interested in the dance, cards were provided in the smaller rooms opening off the ballroom and in the rotunda below the stairs.

The special train provided for Port Arthur guests brought a large number of interested friends in time for the grand promenade at 9:30. Numbers of out-of-town guests, some of them former residents of the city, were also noticed among the throngs.

The Boy Scouts in their uniforms did splendid service and the women workers will not soon forget their courteous and polite attention to guests. They were in charge of F. Jones, the Scoutmaster, and the staff was composed of: Jack Fryer, leader "Ravens"; C. Hind, leader "Scals"; F. McKen, leader "Wolves"; C. Cuthbert, F. Edwards of "Ravens"; B. Humphreys, "Scals"; Gerald North, W. Robinson, Stanley Birdsall, "Wolves".

The refreshments were served from the newsstand and the large tables spread before the stand. The members of the committee were assisted in serving by many of the young ladies present, the workers of the Ladies Aid, and also by the Boy Scouts.

The festivities were kept up till an early hour this morning and with such a brilliant opening the new station should stand for much in the achievement and progress of the city.

Prince Arthur Hotel

Prince Arthur Hotel on Cumberland Street, c 1911 (Collection EAW)

Year Built: 1911
Architect: J.D. Matheson
Style: Chicago Style
Heritage Status: 'Non-Designated' Heritage Property (City of Thunder Bay)

The Prince Arthur Hotel, like its older sibling—the Canadian National Railway Station at the Marina—were both born of the railway. Although the hotel's conception was, one could say, a bit more spontaneous—in that it involved a poker game. *Unfortunately*, the story is not that shady.

The story goes, that in 1908, the Mayor of Port Arthur, J.J. Carrick, and the President of the CNR, Sir William Mackenzie, were playing poker aboard Mackenzie's private rail car enroute to Winnipeg. At one point in the night, who knows how many Scotch Whiskys later, Carrick offered Mackenzie prime land on Cumberland Street if the railway would build a hotel. Mackenzie immediately accepted Carrick's offer and promised to spend $250,000: he more than kept his word, and in the end the CNR spent $500,000 to build the hotel (roughly the equivalent of $9,000,000 today). This deal made the Prince Arthur the first hotel in the CNR's elite chain of railway hotels, later joined by the Chateau Laurier in Ottawa, Jasper Park Lodge in Alberta, and The Bessborough in Saskatoon. The CNR later sold the hotel to private ownership.

The Lobby, c 1911 (Collection TLS)

When the Prince Arthur Hotel opened in 1911, it took its place as one of the most luxurious hotels in Canada. An Edwardian tourist would have been pleased to find a grand piano in the drawing room and the bellboys dressed in nicely pressed green and gold uniforms. The CNR also brought in their resident landscape artist, Mr. H. F. Boyce, who designed a beautiful terraced garden that cascaded from the east door down to Water Street. Remember, these were the days when visitors came to Port Arthur and Fort William by rail or ship, thus there was no need for an unsightly parking lot.

Opening day at the hotel was a grand event with over 100 prominent guests sitting down to enjoy one of the finest meals ever served in Port Arthur. Even by today's standards, the menu's eighteen courses are an epicurean feast:

Caviar Canape a la Russe
Blue Points on Shell
Essence of Tomatoes En Tasse
Stuffed Celery, Radishes, Olives
Sherry

Medallions of Halibut, Sauce Valois
Pommes Dauphine
Tournedos of Beef Tenderloin, Bernaise Sauce
Pomme Pailles, Haricots, Flageolets
Claret

Punch Benedictine
Supreme of Chicken with Fresh Mushrooms
New Potatoes in Cream
Champagne

Salad Prince Arthur
Cheese Souffle
Demi-Tasse
Cognac

I have to admit, I had to go to my *Joy of Cooking* to find out what half of the items on the menu were: in case you are in the same predicament, let me save you a trip. *Sauce Valois* is Bernaise Sauce with beef extract; *Pommes Dauphine* are mashed potatoes mixed with a puff pastry batter and then fried; *Pommes Pailles* are thinly sliced fried potatoes; a *Tournedo of Beef* is a small round slice of beef taken from the end of the tenderloin; and *Punch Benedictine* is a potent mixture of tea, sugar, white burgundy wine, Benedictine liqueur, seltzer and fruit juices.

Dining Room, scene of the opening day luncheon, c 1915 (Canada Science and Technology Museum, Ottawa)

The ambiance of the meal was optimistic and jovial, as captured in the following article, *Luncheon At Opening of Hotel Enjoyable Function,* a fascinating glimpse into Port Arthur's heady early days. Read along as the reporter conveniently punctuates the speeches with '*Cheers*', '*Loud Cheers*', '*Laughter*' and '*Loud Laughter*'. And read between the lines as city officials from Port

Arthur and Fort William throw good–natured jibes back and forth. In honour of the occasion, and in keeping with historical accuracy, I suggest you pour yourself a glass of sherry, claret, champagne or cognac, to toast along with the guests.

Port Arthur Daily News, March 15, 1911

LUNCHEON AT OPENING OF HOTEL ENJOYABLE FUNCTION

Several Excellent Speeches in Which Optimism Abounded—One Hundred Prominent People Guests of the Canadian Northern

Yesterday which was described by one of the speakers at the luncheon as an epoch-making day in the history of Port Arthur, the magnificent new Canadian Northern hotel, the Prince Arthur, was opened for the public.

By a happy thought on the part of the railway executive, the throwing open of this, the handsomest house of rest between Toronto and Vancouver, with the exception of the Royal Alexandra, Winnipeg, which latter does not surpass the Prince Arthur in wealth of equipment or perfection of detail, was made memorable by a bounteous spread, such as only the leading hotels of the largest cities in Canada and the United States furnish.

The luncheon was given free of charge by the Canadian Northern railway to over 100 guests, who comprised the leading men in municipal and business

life in Port Arthur, representatives of the press from Winnipeg and the twin cities of Port Arthur and Fort William, and railway men prominent in the operating life of the company which has made Port Arthur its headquarters and which yesterday opened its first transcontinental hotel in Canada, the Hotel Prince Arthur being the first and strongest link in a chain of hotels that within a few years will stretch from coast to coast.

Optimism a Feature

The spirit of optimism, enthusiasm and future development marked the tone of every speech delivered, both by the railway officials and every speaker who addressed the large gathering. A new note was struck of co-operation between Port Arthur and Fort William which will one day form the tonic of a major chord which will sing as one voice the magic word 'Union' when the two growing cities at the head of the lakes will be brought together as one huge metropolis.

Of the luncheon itself nothing can be said but the words of the highest praise. Everything was prepared by the hands of the most experienced chef that has ever served up a meal in Port Arthur. The reinforced staff of waiters attended to every want of the guests, in many cases anticipating their needs.

The choicest hothouse flowers graced the tables, while the wines and liqueurs were beyond criticism.

Grill Room, c 1911 (Collection TLS)

1901—'The Last Spike'

The occasion took back the mind of the writer of this article, as it must have reverted the minds of many present, to another similar banquet given over nine years ago at the Mariaggi Hotel in honour of Messrs. Mackenzie and Mann, when the last spike was driven in the right of way between Winnipeg and Port Arthur on the Canadian Northern railway, this linking up Port Arthur with the capital of the west by another great railway.

The spike of silver was prepared by a Port Arthur mining engineer, Mr. F.N. Gibbs, and was driven near Slate River. At that time, in December 1901, there was the same feeling of jubilation over work well done, but even the most enthusiastic prophet could not have foretold that well within 10 years, in less than a decade, an Epicurean luncheon would be served in the same company's own hotel, a veritable palace within Port Arthur's own demesne when every utterance was pregnant with optimistic meaning and promise for the future.

Mr. George H. Shaw, traffic manager of the Canadian Northern Railway, presided at the luncheon, and acted as toastmaster in a very acceptable manner.

Mr. G.H. Shaw

After the loyal toast of the King had been universally drunk and musically honoured, Mr. Shaw said that no one regretted more than he did the absence of Mr. Hugh Sutherland at that luncheon. He had really intended to be present, but was detained in Winnipeg for business reasons....

In Port Arthur and Fort William they had strategic points in regard to interprovincial traffic, and it remained with the citizens of both places to attract tourists and other traffic thither. (*Cheers.*)....

Through Line Shortly

"We will have," said Mr. Shaw, "within five years a through line in operation. It may not be within your knowledge that we are operating nearly 1,000 miles of railway in eastern Canada at present time, and we hope to be operating between the Niagara peninsula and Quebec within a year.

"The time has not yet come to place a fleet of high class steamers on the great lakes, but that will come as the natural order of things in the development of our system.

"We have Trans-Atlantic steamers, none better, though some may be larger, and you will be pleased to hear that the patronage we are receiving is more than we ever expected to get. We hope that the opening of this hotel will mark a new era in the development of the Twin Ports. I am satisfied that under the management of Mr. McLean and the supervision of Mr. Pratt, with whom I have been associated for 20 years, the travelling public will have no fault to find with the accommodation they will receive at this house.

Other Plans

"We hope to erect a tourist hotel at Fort Frances at an early date. When that building is complete and our line is opened between Duluth and Virginia, we hope that we will be able to attract tourist travel which adds so much to a community. If the Twin Ports will only work together, I am satisfied that none of you can foresee the future of the prosperity of the ports at the head of the lakes." (*Loud cheers.*)

Toast—"The Twin Ports"

With the toast of the Twin Ports were coupled the names of Mayor Ray of Port Arthur and Alderman H. Harkness, acting mayor of Fort William.

CN poster advertising the SS *Noronic* (built in Port Arthur in 1913) and the Prince Arthur Hotel, part of its steamship-railway link on the Great Lakes, c. 1915 (Toronto Public Library).

Mayor Ray, who on rising received an ovation, said in the course of his remarks that one of the distinguishing features about the people of Port Arthur was their hospitality. Such a feeling was good for tourists and strangers when they came to a city. Whenever Mr. Shaw came to Port Arthur people always welcomed him as a friend. (*Cheers.*)

If the two cities of Port Arthur and Fort William would combine they would become a very large city: if they did not they would still in the future become great cities.

Port Arthur dated its propserity from the day when Mackenzie and Mann applied for a charter in the west. That era of prosperity had reached its present height when the Prince Arthur Hotel was built. (*Cheers.*)

The railway company would be compelled very soon to build the two wings on the hotel, one on Arthur Street [Red River Road] and the other on Van Norman Street, because the growing condition of Port Arthur and district would require it.

Nor were they the only growing city in Canada, though they were growing rapidly in size and in importance. The worst they could wish for the new hotel was that it would have to be trebled in size very soon. Port Arthur hoped to attract not only industries but tourists. The best money that was brought into a place was tourist money.

For ten years the C.N.R. had been growing, so had the city of Port Arthur. The city's assessment was 11 times greater today than it was ten years ago: the population was now three times as great. Who could foresee what it might be in ten years from now?

Around the head of the lakes there would be, in ten years, more than 100,000 people, perhaps nearly double that amount. (*Cheers.*)

Port Arthur Industrial Centre

As the west was growing so rapidly Port Arthur was destined to be the centre of industries, because here they could manufacture the raw material. "One time," said the mayor, "we lived upon the growth of Fort William: what do you think of that? We were glad to do so because they got the railroad. We look to the C.N.R. to co-establish other industries here."

Alderman Harkness

Acting Mayor H. Harkness, of Fort William, replying to the same toast, said that in building a hotel at Port Arthur the C.N.R. had made a good choice and chosen a good spot. Thirty-one years ago the place was known as Prince Arthur's Landing, and now here was the Prince Arthur Hotel.

"The time is coming," said the speaker, "when the two cities are going to love one another."

Mayor Ray—"Oh you awful flirt!" (*Loud laughter.*) "They are called twins," continued Mr. Harkness, amid renewed laughter, "but I wish to God there had been only one born instead of two."

The gardens at the Prince Arthur Hotel, c 1915 (Collection EAW)

Joint Commercial Interests

Received amid scenes of intense enthusiasm was the next toast.... Linked with this toast were the names of Mr. George Graham president of the Board of Trade, Fort William, and Mr. F.S. Wiley, president of the Port Arthur Board of Trade, Mr. Graham said that the one special interest upon which Port Arthur and Fort William should join, if on no other, was power.

They should combine to develop their water powers, for they should have cheaper power for all industries than they were getting in both cities.

"I believe," said Mr. Graham, "that the rivalry that once existed had got down to a reasonable basis. Nobody living in Port Arthur would attempt to keep anything from Fort William next to getting it for their own city.

"Fort William, I believe, wants to see Port Arthur prosper. Nothing but grass growing in the streets of the other place was once upon a time suitable for either of us. (*Laughter.*)

"If anyone lost a cow in Fort William we would tell him to go to Port Arthur and see if the missing animal was grazing on the streets. (*Laughter.*)

"Happily this is all changed and neither city is a menace to the other."

Delightful Contrast

Mr. F.S. Wiley said the present luncheon was a delightful contrast to his first introduction to Port Arthur. He came there in 1872, and there was a banquet going on on the day of his arrival.

On that day it was on the shores of Thunder Bay in an old log cabin. They had a larger bill of fare than was put before them at the luncheon they had just enjoyed. They dined on buffalo tongue, beaver tails and porcupine steaks. (*Laughter.*)

He thought it was a good thing to attract tourists and capital. With the realization of that, the hotel had in sight both tourists and capital from Great Britain and the Orient.

He did not wish to disparage the other hotels in Port Arthur. In the building of the Mariaggi and Algoma hotels they had met the requirements so far, but the city had developed to such an extent that they required something more, and that they had got it in the Prince Arthur.

In a few years they would have to double their capacity. People had come from the east and west and found it so impossible to get the accommodations they required in Port Arthur that they had not stopped over, and the capitalists who were seeking investment had passed by Port Arthur because they could find no place to stop.

Land Not Given Away

A great many people had thought when Port Arthur gave that land for a hotel to the C.N.R. that they were giving away a birthright. They would find that the company had spent $300,000 on the building and before they had finished they would have spent close on half a million.

These returns the railway company were going to get out of that investment would redound to the benefit of everyone at the head of the lakes.

"You all know," said Mr. Wiley, "that we have the greatest climate in the world for six months in the year (A voice—*"Twelve months."*)

"The railways are charging a very high rate to bring people into the head of the lakes. The Boards of Trade of Port Arthur and Fort William should urge upon the railways the lowering of their rates.

"Let them reduce their rates and make these places the attractive spots they should be." (Chorus from the steamship men—*"Let 'em come by lake."*)

"We have here all kinds of birds, all kinds of game, moose, deer and caribou, so it is up to the railways to bring people in at reasonable rates."

In conclusion Mr. Wiley touched upon the recent merger of the Northern Navigation Company into the Richelieu and Ontario boat interests. That meant that people would be carried from Montreal and Quebec through into New Ontario and return (A voice—*"We don't want them to return."*) that had never been accomplished in the past.

The toast of the press was responded to by Mr. G.H. Saults of the Winnipeg Free Press and Mr. F.B. Allen of Port Arthur.

'The Canadian Northern Railway' toast had coupled to it the names of Superintendent A. Wilcox and Mr. Walter Pratt Jr., both of whom replied in neat speeches and the final toast heartily honoured and gracefully responded to 'The Chairman'. Mr. G.H. Shaw brought a never-to-be-forgotten luncheon to a close.

Whalen Building

Whalen Building, 1915 (*Atlantic Terra-Cotta* Vol II: 4)

Year Built: 1913
Architect: Brown and Vallance of Montreal
Style: Chicago Skyscraper
Heritage Status: City of Thunder Bay Heritage Property

"James Whalen had faith in Port Arthur—he built an eight–storey office building in a two–storey town," said Port Arthur's Mayor at the 1941 unveiling of a plaque dedicated to James Whalen at the southwest corner of his famous building.

You have probably passed by this building many times, yet you may not know the Whalen Building's story (also called the PUC Building or the Hydro Building). We'll start with the man who built it: James Whalen. In his time, James Whalen (1869-1929) was one of Port Arthur's greatest 'boosters' and one of the most optimistic men in town—boldly declaring that Port Arthur would one day become the 'Chicago of the North'.

In 1911, he was making a fortune through his marine empire. His two biggest companies included the Western Dry Dock and Shipbuilding Company (later the Port Arthur Shipbuilding Company)—which built the 600–person passenger steamship the *Noronic* in 1913, the largest and most luxurious passenger ship on the Great Lakes; and the Great Lakes Dredging Company, which owned an impressive fleet of 20 boats, including his namesake, the tugboat the *James Whalen*. He also owned the Lyceum Theatre on Cumberland Street, a zinc mine and a logging operation, to name a few of his enterprises.

The Whalen building is a reflection of James Whalen's optimism and enthusiasm. Unlike bland box–stores today, the Whalen Building gives the eye a lot to take in. If you look closely, you will notice the terra–cotta facade is carved with a variety of reliefs, ranging from pelicans to lions to floral designs. Some of the reliefs make sense, for example, some are patriotic symbols of the British Empire (the lions) or of Canada (the provincial crests). Others are less obvious, for instance, what does the pelican symbolize? It helps to know that many of these carvings are not unique to the Whalen Building, but appear on other buildings designed by the architects Brown and Vallance; presumably it was cheaper to reuse the models between their projects. The pelican model (see next page) was probably reused from another building (Vervoort, 1989).

Name panel over central main entrance

Terra-cotta details from the Whalen Buildling, 1915 (*Atlantic Terra-Cotta*, Vol II: 4)

Unfortunately, the Whalen's most elaborate carvings have long been taken down. It is too bad we can't admire the four–foot figures that once graced the corners of the building (see next page)—one was a male figure who resembled either a Scotsman in a kilt or a Roman warrior with a staff, the other was a female figure who wore a long robe and carried a staff.

But we can still admire some of the most intriguing features of the Whalen's facade—the carved human faces. There are eight different faces, which local historian Patricia Vervoort identifies as follows: a 'voyageur', identified by his pipe and beret; a hatless man with a goatee, nicknamed 'Uncle Sam'; a 'Scandinavian' who wears a heavy beard and decorative band; a 'Dutchman' wearing a trilby hat and heavy moustache; an 'Englishman' who sports a slight smile and top hat; a grumpy-looking 'Scotsman' with a tam and thistle; an equally grumpy-looking 'Irishman' with a pipe; and a woman sometimes identified as 'Eve' or 'Ceres', the goddess of agriculture.

Local legend suggests these are the faces of prominent local pioneers, however, to date, no evidence has surfaced that ties the faces to local personalities.

Moving inside, we find an equally sensory–rich interior. No expense was spared for the terrazzo floor, the mahogany doors and window sills, or the marble and polished terra–cotta staircase in the lobby. It feels like you are walking into a museum rather than an office building.

It is safe, and sad, to say that another building like the Whalen Building will never be built in Thunder Bay again. But I am at least glad that the building is widely recognized as one of the city's pre-eminent architectural jewels.

The presence of the Whalen Building reminds us of the importance of *beauty* and *craftsmanship* in one's surroundings. As I read through the building's architectural descriptions and searched out old photos, I began to wonder if as a society we are missing out on something when we don't make *beauty* and *craftsmanship* a priority in our surroundings.

Four-foot figures flanking second story corner widows

Terra-cotta details from the Whalen Building, 1915 (*Atlantic Terra-Cotta* Vol II: 4)

Is it crazy to wonder if ugly buildings (read soulless box–stores or cookie–cutter fast food restaurants) have an adverse effect on our well–being?

Perhaps. But then I came across a study done by Abraham H. Maslow and Norbett L. Mintz in 1956, and I felt like I was onto something. In their study, the researchers compared the responses of subjects in 'beautiful', 'ugly' and 'average' rooms. Subjects were told they were participating in a study that scored the photographs of ten faces for their levels of 'energy' and 'well–being'. The experiments took place in one of the three room types, and each subject was tested in each of the rooms over a period of three weeks.

The beautiful room was decorated to look like a 'comfortable study' with a mahogany desk, a comfortable armchair, wooden bookshelves, a large Navajo rug, pleasant drapes, paintings on the wall and soft lighting. The ugly room was painted battleship grey, had an uncovered, harsh light, a small desk with tin cans for ashtrays, dirty trash–cans, and torn drapes. The average room looked like a 'worked–in' professor's office with a mahogany desk, metal bookcase, metal filing cabinet, and adequate lighting and window shades.

The results strongly suggest environment matters. The researchers found that individuals in the beautiful room gave significantly higher ratings to the ten photographs for energy and well–being than when they were in the ugly room. Subjects were more likely to rate the faces higher for fatigue and sickness in the ugly room. And not only that, but the two examiners, who also didn't know the true nature of the experiment, complained more often of "monotony, fatigue, headache, sleepiness, discontent, irritability, hostility, and avoidance" in the ugly room. Maslow and Mintz reported that when the examiners were told the true nature of the experiment: "They evidenced surprise at the whole procedure...*They were not aware that their activities [complaints] were in such close relationship to the room conditions*, though they both realized that they did not prefer to test in the downstairs [ugly] room." (Italics added.)

In other words, battleship grey walls are detrimental to your health, even if you don't know it!

Although Thunder Bay did not become the 'Chicago of the North', in fact soon after the building was finished the economy nose–dived, the First World War came along, and James Whalen lost all of his money out West. Still, there is something comforting in knowing that the Whalen Building has outlasted all of these disappointments. That such a beautiful building not only carries us forward, but reminds us that it doesn't hurt to be optimistic every once in awhile.

The original mahogany doors of the Whalen Building, Cumberland Street entrance, c 1930. They were replaced by aluminum doors in 1962. (Thunder Bay Archives)

Girls playing in front of the Whalen Building, Cumberland Street entrance (these doors were closed over by 1920). It looks like they are admiring the building's terra-cotta reliefs. c 1915 (Collection EAW)

The Need For Roots

To know who you are, you have to have a place to come from.

Carson McCullers, The Heart is a Lonely Hunter

Earlier I mentioned that roots were important, now I'll explain why. Wherever you are right now, whether that be Thunder Bay or elsewhere, imagine you have roots growing out of the bottom of your feet. How far down into the ground do they go? Barely an inch? A couple of feet? Or do they go down for miles and miles?

Having roots is feeling attached to a place; as Edward Relph (1976) explains: "a familiary that is part of knowing and being known *here*, in this particular place." You may not live at that place anymore, but you go back to your roots, if only in your mind, when you need an anchor. It is that place of comfort that shelters you through the storms of life.

Simone Weil (1955) argues that being attached to a place is one of our most essential human needs. Read Weil's words slowly, perhaps two or three times, letting them sink in:

> To be rooted is perhaps the most important and least recognized need of the human soul. It is one of the hardest to define. A human being has roots by virtue of his real, active and natural participation in the life of the community, which preserves in living shape certain particular expressions for the future. This participation is a natural one in the sense that it is automatically brought about by place, conditions of birth, profession and social surroundings. Every human being needs to have multiple roots. It is necessary for him to draw well-nigh the whole of his moral, intellectual and spiritual life by way of the environment of which he forms a part.

But that is not all. The places that we are most attached to, are the places that we also *care* the most about. That means you will care about whether or not the place you love is torn down or still standing; whether a favourite street has more or less empty storefronts; or whether your hometown is doing better or worse than the last time you saw it: "to care for a place involves more than having a concern for it that is based on certain past experiences and future expectations—there is also a real responsibility and respect for that place both for itself and for what it is to yourself and others" (Relph, 1976).

Not surprisingly, some of the places we are most attached to are historic buildings. Some simply by way of their longevity in our lives. All relationships are built on 'redundancy', meaning we need to have many interactions with an individual over time before we are familiar with them and consider them a friend. Our relationships with historic buildings may work in the same way. Other historic buildings may find their way into our hearts because of their architectural beauty or because we have intimate relationships with them as our schools, libraries or churches.

This sense of deep care for places is not only essential for our mental health, but for the health of our communities. One of the best things a community can do for itself is to foster this kind of caring in its citizens. But this relationship is not static. We can become *uprooted* if this care is not fostered.

Indeed, it is uprooting to see more and more familiar places, places where we once lived or went to school, become vacant lots. It is like having the rug pulled out from under you over and over again. Our discomfort stems from the fact that places are the memory-keepers for our stories and memories, and, it is our memories that anchor our identity. "Identity is intimately tied to memory," writes Dolores Hayden in *The Power of Place*:

> Both our personal memories (where we have come from and where we have dwelt) and the collective or social memories interconnect with the histories of our families, neighbors, fellow workers, and ethnic communities. Urban landscapes are storehouses for these social memories, because natural features such as hills or harbours, as well as streets, buildings, and patterns of settlement, frame the lives of many people and often outlast many lifetimes.

It makes sense then, that if we lose these familiar places; we begin to lose access to our memories (Casey, 1987; Cresswell and Hoskins, 2008). And if we lose access to our memories, we lose our sense of identity. David Lowenthal writes in *The Past is a Foreign Country*, that "the past is integral to our sense of identity; the sureness of 'I was' is a necessary component of the sureness of 'I am.'"

We need to be aware that there are consequences to living in a society where individuals have lost their sense of identity. If we stop caring about the place we live, we lose our sense of community, and society becomes fragmented. We would do well to heed Simone Weil's warning: "Whoever is uprooted himself uproots others. Whoever is rooted himself doesn't uproot others."

I've selected the buildings in this next section because they are good 'rooting' buildings. Some are probably buildings that you already have a relationship with, such as your school, church or library; or they are places where people come together in fellowship, like the Masonic Hall. Or places we have a soft spot for, even if we don't know why, like the Pagoda. The presence of these buildings in our neighbourhoods helps form those key connections we need to be fully human and ultimately root us in the place we live.

Pagoda

The Pagoda, 2007 (Photo EAW)

Year Built: 1909
Architect: H. Russell Halton
Style: 'Eclectic Thunder Bay'
Heritage Status: National Historic Site

"It will be an ugly thumb in the middle of downtown."
Councillor John Ranta, *Chronicle Journal*, Nov 8, 1988

"Tear it down: get rid of it. It's of little historical interest—nothing happened there. And, apart from a few sentiments, no one cares about it."
Councillor Joe Vanderwees, *Chronicle Journal*, Feb 6, 1987

"It's a pile of junk. Take a can of gas to it…it's just splinters of wood that are so dislocated it would take a magician to fix it."
Councillor Sterling Lysnes, *Lakehead Living*, Nov 9, 1988

This is the story of the little building that could. The Pagoda is *the* iconic building in Thunder Bay, but in the 1980s it barely escaped the wrecker's ball. Can you imagine the city without the Pagoda? It almost happened.

The Pagoda's story—of being one of the most celebrated buildings in Thunder Bay to being voted 9-3 in *favour* of demolition—should be a lesson to us all about what *not* to do. It is a lesson about what happens when a city forgets its history.

Origins

It all started in 1909, when a short article appeared in the *Port Arthur Daily News* challenging the Port Arthur City Council to 'beautify' the city:

Without going to the expense of erecting an Arch of Triumph or a Statue of Liberty, it is possible that a few dollars might be expended in improving these surroundings with profit to the city.

The *next* day City Council placed an advertisement on the front page of the newspaper requesting sketches from architects for a building to be called The 'Pagoda'. The Pagoda would be a monument to Port Arthur's civic pride and an attraction for tourists. The adjudication committee made it clear they were looking for something out of the ordinary:

The merits of the sketches submitted are to be judged by their appropriateness to express clearly to the stranger the peculiar characteristics of the District of Thunder Bay, as it is intended to construct and furnish the building entirely of native materials...It should breathe publicity, radiate hope, and shriek: P-O-R-T---A-R-T-H-U-R. The object of the building of the Pagoda is chiefly to attract to the city the attention of tourists and the general travelling public.

Architectural drawing of the Pagoda, 1909 (*Port Arthur Daily News*)

The existence of the Pagoda will furnish a reasonable cause to warrant the investigation of every traveller. The Pagoda, as proposed, will be manned by some person authorized to speak for the city, distribute descriptive literature, talk up Port Arthur, extend this freedom of the city to visitors and make the stranger feel that his presence is welcome.

The deadline was less than a week later, and five architects submitted their proposals. The winner was H. Russell Halton, a local architect who had also designed the Lyceum Theatre. The newspaper described his design as "a building of simple octagonal design, with a canopy roof and a tower". Simple! We'll get back to that.

The whole town got behind the project. The City Council of Port Arthur approved $2,500 for its construction and the *Port Arthur Daily News* reported a list of local companies that offered to provide services and supplies *free* of cost:

Messrs. Steward & Hewitson, The Marks, Clavet, Dobie Company, Wells and Emmerson, Vigars Shear Lumber company and Pigeon River Lumber Company have offered to supply, free of cost, various parts of the material required....and Mr. Antonio Pella will lay the handsome Mosaic floor, also without remuneration for his work.

Even a City Councillor was willing to work for free:

Alderman McRae has agreed to personally supervise the work of the construction without remuneration.

All of this goodwill helped speed construction along. From the time the call for drawings was made in April 1909, to the opening reception in February 1910, the Pagoda was conceived, designed and built in only 10 months.

The Pagoda, 1925. On its right is the Daily News Building, just behind it, the top of the CN Station can be seen. (National Archives)

What Was The Architect Thinking?

The Pagoda was never supposed to be a wallflower. The original idea was to create an exotic building that people would talk about and which would bring publicity to the town. By these criteria the Pagoda has succeeded.

But the Pagoda is definitely confusing to look at. It combines an eclectic mix of Indian, Scandinavian, Canadian, Greek and Roman architectural styles. And although one's first impression may be that it is funny looking, the Pagoda's unconventional combination of styles might actually have deeper symbolic meaning.

The following description, from the 1977 report of the *Local Architectural Conservation Advisory Committee*, explains how the seemingly disjointed architectural styles of the Pagoda may actually be representative of the multi-cultural nature of the city:

> It is moreover appropriate that the Pagoda is in Thunder Bay rather than anywhere else, since stylistically the building is symbolic of Thunder Bay's geographical location in Canada—the place where East meets West. The Pagoda itself is a building in which styles from the East and West meet. The roof of the Pagoda is called a 'chatri' roof, the defining characteristic being its umbrella shape. This kind of roof is typical of Islamic architecture in India. The columns around the building supporting the roof form what is called a peristyle; that is the name for an outer colonnade surrounding a building. The peristyle is Greek in origin and is a basic type of structure for Western European architecture. The little ornament over the gable of the entranceway is Scandinavian in origin; it is reminiscent of carved dragon's heads found on medieval structures in Norway and Finland. The pilaster (the flat column) on either side of the entranceway are Roman in origin, and of course, the panel with the beaver puts the Canadian stamp on the building.

A further note about that beaver. When I first noticed the beaver—which was carved by a local sculptor named Mr. B. Jones out of Bedford, Indiana stone—I thought he looked, well, rather angry. But then I came across this amusing description of the beaver published in the *Port Arthur Daily News* (July 22, 1909) and I realized my mistake:

The panel…represents a colossal beaver actively engaged in tearing the bark of a log, preparatory to building its home and helping in the work of erecting dams in the beaver colony.

The beaver wasn't having a bad day, he was just busy!

Beaver panel on the Pagoda, 2008. (Photo TLS)

How the Pagoda Got Its Spots

On Sunday June 25, 1961 the residents of Port Arthur woke up to find polka dots had been painted on their Pagoda. The whole roof was covered in red, yellow, pink and blue polka dots. Who in the world would have done such a thing? Nobody owned up.

At first, the Port Arthur Chamber of Commerce announced that the dots would be removed immediately. But then, the national media got a hold of the story, and the Pagoda's picture was splashed across the front pages of national newspapers. Visitor traffic to the building was up 63%.

Now the polka dots didn't seem like such a bad idea and city officials backed down on their threats to paint over them.

So, who was responsible? And how did they carry out such an ambitious plan without anybody knowing about it?

It all happened in the wee hours of Sunday June 25, 1961, when eight young members of the Thunder Bay Jaycees, ranging in ages from 26 to 34, secured their ladders to the Pagoda and climbed up. Contrary to legend, they were actually found out right away. A concerned citizen spied the painters, and presuming they were up to no good, called the police.

The Pagoda, c 1961. The old CPR station is in the background. (Collection EAW)

The police came by to investigate and took down the names of the eight men, but they let them carry on. As one member of the polka dot brigade later explained: "The police came down with a paddy wagon and it took a lot of explaining but I guess they thought we were crazy enough to be really pulling off a publicity stunt, so they left us to our work." (*Lakehead Living, July 22 1981.*) The dots stayed on for two decades, and then in

1980, were painted over. But only a year later, the Jaycees were again involved in painting the dots back on the Pagoda. This time it was a much less scandalous affair, in broad daylight, with full approval of tourism officials. The dots have since been repainted over.

9-3 In *Favour* Of Demolition

After reading all of the above, and knowing that the Pagoda was the first building in Thunder Bay to be designated a local Heritage Building in 1979, it seems hard to believe that in 1988 City Council voted 9-3 to tear it down. But it's true: in 1988, the majority of Councillors voted to erase 80 years of history. But it gets even worse. At the same meeting, some of the Councillors who voted to tear down the Pagoda actually proposed that the city should build a replica of it in the Marina.

Councillor Dusty Miller, who voted against demolition, shot back: "Building a replica is historically meaningless."

And Councillor Betty Kennedy, who also voted against demolition, replied: "I think this is one of the biggest wastes of taxpayers' money I've seen on this council. I see no point in a replica and I don't care where you put it."

(Both quotes are from the *Chronicle Journal*, Nov 8, 1988)

The only thing that gave the Pagoda a bit of breathing space between the vote and the wrecking ball was that under the Heritage Act the City could not demolish the Pagoda without a three-month delay. This gave the forces working to save the Pagoda a little more time. The three Councillors who voted against demolition, Dusty Miller, David Hamilton and Betty Kennedy, became its most passionate defenders.

Local people also became involved. A grass-roots fundraising organization called *Friends of The Pagoda* was formed and members of the *Local Architectural Conservation Advisory Committee* were vocal opponents. Many editorials and Letters to the Editor implored City Council not to tear down the Pagoda.

When council resumed again in early 1989, Councillor Miller wasn't going to give up: "I think there's a strong possibility we can get seven votes for Pagoda restoration. I'll be darned if I'll admit defeat at this stage." (*Chronicle Journal*, Feb 4, 1989.)

Good thing she didn't give up.

Saved, By *One* Vote

On February 13, 1989, Councillor Miller made one last impassioned speech to save the Pagoda. Her speech to City Council was reported in the *Chronicle Journal*:

> "I've had many calls from people who feel very strongly about this issue," she said.
>
> Miller said one local Second World War veteran, returning home disorientated and joyless from the conflict, told her he did not cheer up 'until he saw the little Pagoda'.
>
> "Whether or not you feel the building is worth much, you must recognize that there are very many people to whom it gives a sense of community."

Councillor Miller got her 7 votes. City Council voted in favour of restoring the Pagoda by the narrowest of margins, 7-6.

Helping to turn the tide were financial pledges from the *Friends of the Pagoda* and the Ontario Heritage Foundation's contribution of $105,000. Later that year, the Pagoda was made a *National Historic Site*; one of only three in the city.

"Why Should it Matter?"

It is clear that many people in Thunder Bay were strongly opposed to tearing down the Pagoda. Why? If it was just "an ugly thumb", "a pile of junk"? Why not build a replica?

By now it should be clear: because historic buildings root us. They remind us of who we are, of our stories, and the stories of our parents and grandparents. Buildings are the physical embodiment of our memories; and, as wrote Saul Bellow, we need our memories "to keep the wolf of insignificance from the door."

Buildings tie us to the past in a way that no other experience can. In 1909, the architect John Ruskin wrote:

> It is well to have not only what men have thought and felt,
> but what their hands have handled,
> and their strength wrought,
> and their eyes beheld,
> all the days of their life.

In other words, we literally need to touch the past.

We also need to be rooted-*forward*. Sigfried Giedion (1962) calls this the *demand for continuity*. He writes: "It has become apparent that human life is not limited to a single lifespan but goes far beyond. It is impossible to sever its contacts with the past as to prevent its contacts with the future. Something lives within us which forms part of the very backbone of human dignity: I call this the demand for continuity."

In other words, I need to know, that you know, that *I was here*.

In Thunder Bay, my generation has seen whole neighbourhoods bulldozed in the name of progress (South Cumberland Street), other areas slide into neglect (Simpson Street, Victoria Street, McKellar Park), and historic buildings 'replaced' by gaping holes (Cornwall Avenue School). In many cases these changes have happened with relatively little consultation, or outcry. Decades later we know we are missing something, but we don't quite know what. Melissa Holbrook Pierson sums up this disquiet in *The Place You Love is Gone*:

> We are a generation weighted down by a sadness we do not know we feel... What is lost was here just thirty or forty years ago, and thus it is written all over the page of your life. But still you don't know what can be done. Each announcement comes wrapped in its own fait accompli: this going, this coming, look away, cry alone, it's done. The golf courses, the roads, the stores, the cutting, drilling, stripping.

We are fooling ourselves if we think we have escaped the wrecking ball unscathed, when in fact, these losses have had an effect on us. Rather than assume there will be no consequences, we should assume there *will* be consequences when our favourite buildings are demolished.

Perhaps we need to think about the deterioration of our built environment in the same way we think about the deterioration of our natural environment: we can't expect to ruin our natural environment and not suffer the consequences. Likewise, we can't expect to ruin our built environment and come out of it unscathed.

Brodie Street Library

The Brodie Street Library, c 1912 (Collection EAW)

Year Built: 1912
Architect: Hood and Scott
Style: Classical Revival
Heritage Status: City of Thunder Bay Heritage Property

The Brodie Street Library is one of my favourite places in Thunder Bay. Not only is it an architectural treasure, it is a 'great good place'.

Ray Oldenburg coined the term a 'great good place' to describe a place that creates *community*. Great good places are different from your home (your 'first place') and your work (your 'second place'). They are your 'third place'.

Oldenburg defines a third place as a neutral place that is universally accessible to people from all walks of life and can host regular, voluntary gatherings. Third places serve to expand social interactions between people you might not otherwise meet at work or in your neighbourhood or family. They can also be the place you meet your 'regulars', the place you meet your friends for coffee or the members of your book club.

Unfortunately, third places are disappearing from the North American landscape as more and more people live a 'bipodal' life of home and work. Oldenburg laments the loss:

> We sorely need [third places] to construct the infrastructure of human relationships. Life styles are increasingly privatized and competitive; residential areas are increasingly devoid of gathering places. To the extent of our affluence, we avoid public parks, public playgrounds, public schools and public transportation.

But without third places, we demand too much out of the other spheres of our lives, which can lead to disappointment. Writes Oldenburg:

> In the absence of an informal public life, people's expectations toward work and family have escalated beyond the capacity of these institutions to meet them. Domestic and work relationships are pressed to supply all that is wanting and much that is missing in constricted lifestyles of those without community.

With very little fanfare, the library is a much needed third place in the lives of many people. It is a humanizing place where you can simply read your book, check your email, or read the newspaper and have no other expectations of you.

It is one of the few places left where you can spend a couple of hours and not pay a cent.

And not only is the Brodie Street Library a 'great good place' it is such a beautiful 'great good place'. Although the mahogany front doors are gone and the oversized circulation desk has been replaced, the Reading Room retains its turn-of-the-century elegance. It harkens back to a different era, when it was normal for a patron to enjoy his or her book surrounded by oak newspaper racks, a cosy fireplace, and stained glass windows of the likes of Tolstoy, Shakespeare and Burns. It is hard to believe the library, and all of its goodwill, was built for only $50,000—a donation from the Scottish-American steel baron Andrew Carnegie.

Original front entrance with stained glass window of Andrew Carnegie, c 1930 (Thunder Bay Public Library)

The success of the Brodie Street Library would have made Mary J.L. Black proud. Black (1879-1939) was its first librarian and it is on her shoulders that the library owes its success. In 1934, she wrote a very forward thinking article for the *Library Journal* that captures the essence of what a library is all about. Her words remind us that the Brodie Street Library has always encouraged people from all walks of life to find sanctuary and learning in the library, with no other expectation of them. Way back then, before anyone knew what a 'great good place' was, Mary J.L. Black knew that a library was more than a repository for books; it was about helping people find their way in life.

Library Journal, Vol. 59 (June 15, 1934): 510-511

FORT WILLIAM, ONTARIO, PUBLIC LIBRARY

By Mary J.L. Black

In many respects the Fort William Public Library [now the Brodie Street Library] is like scores of other libraries in cities of twenty-five thousand. In appearance it is a typical 'Carnegie Library', and in plan equally conventional.

It was an inexpensive building, but the money was spent unusually wisely, so that now after twenty-two years the building and furniture stand almost as fresh as the day it was opened. Of course, it has pillars and an entrance that occupies far too much room, but having passed through them, one enters a beautiful room that is almost beyond criticism, eighty-seven feet square and broken by a very few partitions. It is a bright and cheery room, and while the librarian may

begrudge the lack of wall shelving, the reading public get great pleasure out of the big low windows, which are available on all sides.

From the charging desk in the centre, supervision can be given to the entire floor unless the crowd is very great. One side is devoted to the children and young people, the latter having their distinct section in which is everything they need for their school work and enough besides to remove any too academic appearance. Here we have many lovely editions of the great novels and plays, and very successful bait have they proven to be to many a reader, old as well as young.

Circulation Desk, c 1930 (Thunder Bay Public Library)

The general reading room is on the opposite side, and equally attractive. It is particularly well equipped with a cosmopolitan collection of periodicals and newspapers, the indices being close at hand for anyone wishing to use them.

The Reading Room, c 1950 (Thunder Bay Public Library)

In the lower storey is a duplicate newspaper room, and smoking room, where chess and checkers may be played. The general experience with such rooms is not good, so one is glad to be able to report that with us, it has never been a problem. It is used constantly by a group who probably would not otherwise come near the building, and particularly in these days of unemployment it has been a great boon.

On this floor, there is a small and not very attractive lecture hall, which is also used a great deal by all kinds of groups. Whenever possible, an effort is made to coordinate their activities with the direct library service that is available upstairs.

This hall is also used for art exhibits which are held from time to time under the auspices of the library. A very definite result can already be seen in the cultural life of the community as fruit of this phase of the library's activity.

For the first fifteen years of the library's existence, the book collection was a thing of joy to everyone. It contained no dead material and it was very representative. This is no longer true for like all libraries we have suffered from lack of funds and we can no longer view our Science and Useful Arts section with pride.

The other departments have not suffered to the same extent and still can serve any ordinary student.

Canadiana is grouped by itself and its extent is a matter of surprise to many. The local papers are kept permanently on file, and everything bearing our Thunder Bay History is preserved.

Fort William sprawls for several miles along the river front and is divided into three very distinct residential areas. Various experiments have been tried to reach the people living at a distance. Collections of books have been placed in the schools, factories, hospitals and fire halls, and ultimately a completely equipped branch was opened in the west end. This has proven a very great success though it has added a financial burden very difficult to carry. The improved service given showed beyond a doubt that deposit stations are of very little educational value unless there is a trained or thoroughly interested person in charge. The books may have been read, but the reading did not get anywhere.

However, it is not in the buildings or books or staff that our Library is unique, but rather, in its peculiar relationship to the public; the public who show such a happy ownership of the Library and its equipment and who turn to it for solutions of their literary problems or problems far removed from ordinary library duties.

This relationship developed by good luck rather than through any special planning. Our building was opened in 1912, in a period of great growth and prosperity. Houses were scarce and board poor, and the bright cheery Library with its flowers, books and pictures was adopted as 'home' by many of these newcomers, and that relationship continues now even with their children.

There was another large group who early learned to turn to the Library in their special need, the new Canadians of non-English origin. The majority of these did very little reading, even in their own tongue let alone in English, but they too were homesick and, soon learning where they would get a sympathetic hearing to their problems, they also turned to the Library as home.

Brodie Street Library (then called the Public Library), c 1912. Fort William's old City Hall is beside it. (Collection EAW)

Some of them ultimately became readers; many of their children are among our best readers, but primarily the Library served to interpret Canadian thought and institutions to a large number who might not otherwise have been touched at all.

Our critics might say the problems these groups brought us did not come within the field of library work, and that we might better have spent our time doing some of the many tasks which we know have been neglected. Perhaps so, but they have taught us the important lesson that in order to get the right book to the right person, it is even more necessary to know people than books.

Masonic Hall

The Masonic Hall, c 1910 (Collection James Kingston)

Year Built: 1910
Architect: Marshall B. Aylesworth
Style: Combination of Georgian and French Renaissance Styles
Heritage Status: Waverley Park Heritage Conservation District

It is an understatement to say that I was impressed when I toured the Masonic Hall on Red River Road. Think of a time in your life when you have had certain expectations of how you thought something would turn out—but then—much to your delight, your expectations were far surpassed. That was the feeling I had when I visited the Masonic Hall.

From the outside, you might not have noticed this large tan-coloured brick building on Red River Road, which actually looks like three different buildings.

The first part of the building, the skinny portion over the lodge entrance, is defined by two marble columns mounted by globe lights. This stunning entrance is pictured on the front cover of the book.

The second portion of the building, to the right of the entrance, looks like it belongs in the French countryside. The main architectural feature of this section is the Mansard roof, a domed roof with two slopes first made popular in France in the 1600s.

The third portion of the building, which is adjacent to the Bank of Montreal, is defined by four pilasters (flattened columns that slightly project from the building) which gives the building a Greek or Roman look. It is a credit to the architect that he found a way to combine three separate looks into a united front.

On a chilly November day, I was the fortunate recipient of a tour of the building by Mr. James Kingston, a Past Master of the Shuniah Lodge. We started the tour in the first floor lobby, and right away I was struck by an unusual highlight: the lobby's floors. I have to explain, because these weren't your usual-looking floors. Below our feet, were floors made of a rich chocolate brown stone that seemed almost too luxurious to walk on. Some stones were dark brown, others more of a cream or tan colour, and some had flecks of burgundy, pale pink or grey. The stone slabs were cut in a variety of differently sized pieces and fit together in a simple, yet elegant, geometrical design. I asked Mr. Kingston what the floor was made of, and much to my surprise, he said: "Nipigon marble". Now, those are two words you do not expect to hear together, I had heard of Nipigon Nylons before, but not this more sophisticated export.

Mr. Kingston assured me the marble carried on throughout the three floors of the staircase, so I eagerly followed away. Next, we walked to the second floor and entered the 'enter-room' or lobby, and off the enter-room, the library. Another wonderful surprise. Stepping into the library was like stepping into a favourite English uncle's reading room, cosy yet grand.

Masonic Hall, 2008 (Photo TLS)

Everything in the library was made of oak. In the centre of the room was a big oak table surrounded by oak chairs. Against one wall were glass-fronted oak cabinets and bookshelves, most of which were original furnishings—picked out by the architect himself in 1911. Against another wall was the requisite fireplace. For a finishing touch, the walls were covered with old black-and-white photographs dating back to the earliest days of the lodge. I thought to myself that this room would make a great place for a bookclub.

Although I was reluctant to leave the library, Mr. Kingston insisted there was more to see, so I followed him across the enter-room to the Lodge Hall.

He was right. When he switched on the lights in the Lodge Hall, it took my brain a couple of minutes to register what my eyes were seeing. I had actually become momentarily disoriented. Had I really stepped into a room with 19-foot Roman vaulted ceilings?

Let's start at the top: the first thing you notice when you step into the room are the ceiling arches, which give the room the appearance of a Roman banquet hall. Next your eye notices the baby-blue fluted pilasters, which are topped by gold-coloured capitals. Another classical detail that has vanished from modern architecture.

The Lodge Hall, 2007 (Photo TLS)

The room was a blend of light and dark colours. The walls were painted a creamy off-white until midway and then covered in a dark blue velvet cloth which blended with a slightly raised platform that ran along the perimeter of the room. This platform is where Lodge members sit during meetings; the

Officers sit in ornamentally-carved wooden chairs in the north, south, east and west corners of the room. Tying it all together is a deep blue rug that gives the room a regal feel. Perhaps the best way to describe this room is to say that it was like the universe had become geographically confused and stuck an ancient temple in the heart of downtown Thunder Bay.

Although I had to be pried out of the Lodge Hall, I was curious to see what I would find next. I was not disappointed; next we toured the handsome Banquet Hall.

Similar to the Lodge Hall, the ceiling of the Banquet Hall was vaulted, but rested on more subtle pilasters. The walls were painted the same creamy off-white as the Lodge Hall and covered with huge oak frames filled with photographs of Past Masters. I would feel very inspired having dinner here.

The Banquet Hall, 2007 (Photo TLS)

After we left the Banquet Hall, we walked to the third floor (all of which is also wheelchair accessible via a motorized chair lift) to tour the two Social Rooms.

The Social Rooms were more informal than the other rooms, although still furnished with original oak chairs and tables. The

Social Rooms are, of course, for socializing after the meetings. The focal point of one of the Social Rooms was a massive antique pool table—a 100 year old, 6 x 12 foot, 6–pocket, slate-bed pool table made by The Brunswick Balke-Collender Company. It looked like it would outweigh an elephant.

Another interesting feature of the room was a framed panoramic map of Port Arthur in 1885—Port Arthur's 'Golden Age'. The map offers a wondeful bird's–eye view of the city, showing the locations of leading hotels, businesses and prominent residences, most of which are long-gone today. The map also depicts two dozen tallships in the harbour and a good amount of smoke coming from Port Arthur's factories, a not-so-subtle advertisement for the town's booming economy.

The Social Rooms were the last stop on my unforgettable tour. As we walked back down the Nipigon marble staircase to the lobby, I was reluctant to leave. It was actually jarring to go back into the 21st century.

Of course, the Masons are the main beneficiaries of their fine-looking surroundings, but the rest of us are also fortunate they have preserved the building's architectural heritage and are willing to share it with us (they give tours for events such as *Doors Open*).

As I compiled the research for this book, I began to realize that some of my favourite historic buildings, and the ones that were in the best shape, were the buildings associated with 'fellowship', people voluntarily coming together in some form or another, such as what happens at the Brodie Street Library, in Church, or the Masonic Hall. It made me appreciate the importance of fellowship in keeping not only a building alive, but also a sense of community.

In the days of virtual access to people on social networking sites and chatrooms, we may think we are part of a 'community', but what do we miss out on when we forego face-to-face meetings for computer interactions? Does our community suffer? For example, the Masons are not only a social group, they also contribute time and money to charitable causes in the city. Do memberships in chatrooms inspire people to get out and help their neighbours? Or have online 'communities' made us more removed from the physical communities we live in?

I'm not sure, although I did find a revealing study about Internet use and sociality done by Statistics Canada (Veenhof, 2006). In this study, the researcher found that heavy Internet users (defined as people who spend more than one hour a day on the Internet, excluding for educational purposes) spend less time socializing than medium and non-users. More specifically, heavy Internet users spend less time in social contact with friends and family, less time participating in active sports, engaging in civic and volunteer activities, less time attending sports events, movies and other entertainment events and less time playing with their kids. Finally, and not surprisingly, heavy Internet users also spend more time alone than medium and non-users.

This study begs the question: what kind of society are we becoming? Although, when you think about it, all it takes is a flick of the switch. The Roman vaulted-ceiling alone would make me turn off my computer and seek out some friendly faces.

Historic Churches

St. Andrew's Roman Catholic Church, 1939. (Thunder Bay Public Library)

St. John the Evangelist Anglican (1884) • Knox United (1889) • St. Thomas' Anglican (1890) • St. Luke's Anglican (1890) • Trinity United (1905) • First Baptist (1908) • St. Paul's Anglican (1908) • St. Andrew's Presbyterian (1909) • Wesley United (1910) • St. Peter's Slovak (1911) • Ukrainian Orthodox Church of the Assumption of the Blessed Virgin Mary (1912) • St. Paul's United (1914) • St. Augustine's Roman Catholic (1915) • Ukrainian Catholic Church of the Transfiguration (1917) • Ukrainian Catholic Church of the Ascension (1918) • St. Andrew's Roman Catholic (1925) • Lakeview Presbyterian (1927) • St. Stephen's Anglican (1928)

My appreciation for historic churches started when I was living in Montreal. On days when I needed a break from the office, I would take long walks to Old Montreal. On one of these walks, I peaked inside the breathtaking Cathedral-Basilica of Mary, Queen of the World; I was mesmerized by my beautiful surroundings and didn't make it back to the office that day. From that point on, I made it a regular habit to take time-outs in historic churches.

Thunder Bay's historic churches have a similar inspiring effect on me: where else can you see such exquisite craftsmanship? It could only have been a labour of love that wrought the hand-hewn, cream-coloured stones from an island off Sibley Peninsula to Trinity United Church, or sculpted the ten marble columns at St. Andrew's Presbyterian Church, or crafted the intricate stained glass windows at St. Paul's Anglican Church.

"God is in the details," said the famous architect Mies van der Rohe; the point is well taken at Thunder Bay's historic churches. This is the kind of beauty that makes you think about your own life and about the kinds of things that are possible through love, friendship, kindness and compassion.

Churches can be a lot of different things to a lot of different people. But one of the most unique features about a church is that it is the physical location where we can collectively celebrate the 'numinous', the mystery of our lives, that rather incomprehensible fact that we were born and exist on this earth. E.A. Sovik describes the numinous as:

> [T]he human awareness that our lives are lived in the presence of a magnificent mystery—awesome, fascinating, ineffable. It is this transcendent mystery which is the holy. The experience of the numinous comes to us all. It is not only the property of poets and mystics. We are led to it when we reflect on such intimate and immanent things as the wonder of the heartbeat or the unfathomable properties of time or the space in which we exist.

Of course the numinous is not restricted to beautiful churches, but there is something about a beautiful church that can bring that feeling to you. As Margaret Visser writes:

> For anyone who is not spiritually allergic to churches, to walk into a beautiful church is to encounter understanding, to hear echoes of the soul's own experiences of epiphany. Such stimulus and concurrence need not involve anything theological. It can be a matter simply of sunlight striking through coloured glass and dappling the wall opposite, of the smell of flowers and lingering hints of incense, of the silent cold of stone, of movements of the soul that respond directly to columns, arches, domes, colouring and carving, or to the memory of the people who have filled this building in the past.

In this busy, materialistic world we live in, we need to allow these thoughts to sweep over us every now and then.

The front doors of St. Paul's United Church, Waverley St., built 1914.
(Photo TLS 2008)

St. Paul's Anglican Church, Ridgeway St., built 1908.
(Photo TLS 2008)

Stained glass window in St. Paul's Anglican Church. (Photo M. Richardson 2006)

Sanctuary of St. Paul's Anglican Church, 2008 (Photo TLS)

Trinity United Church, Algoma St., built 1905. City of Thunder Bay Heritage Property (Photo TLS 2008)

Sanctuary at Trinity United Church, 2008 (Photo TLS)

The Ukrainian Catholic Church of the Transfiguration, McIntosh St., built 1917. 'Non-Designated' Heritage Property. (Photo TLS 2007)

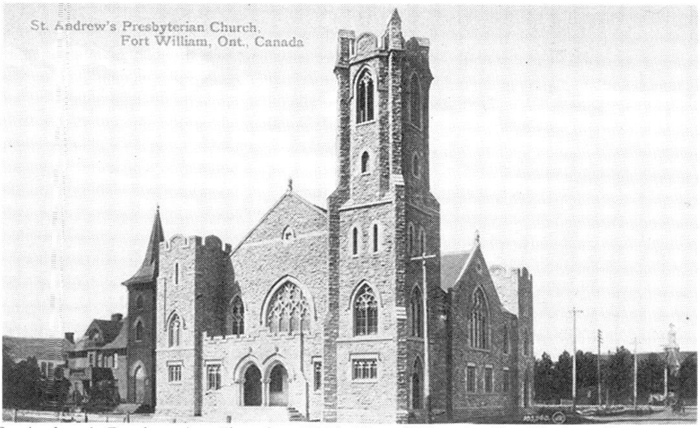

St. Andrew's Presbyterian Church c. 1910. City of Thunder Bay Heritage Property. Left is the original church, it was moved to Pruden Street in 1913 and became Knox United Church (Collection EAW)

Fort William Daily Times Journal, June 12, 1909

ST. ANDREW'S PRESBYTERIAN CHURCH OPEN FOR DEDICATION

"When we build," once said that immortal art critic, John Ruskin, "let it be such work as our descendants will thank us for."

This must have been the ideal towards which the people of St. Andrew's Church were striving when they began to build their magnificent house of worship. All those who come after the present builders of that new church, will hold in grateful remembrance the people who wrought in stone, iron and wood, such a splendid expression of their loyalty and devotion to the cause of Christianity and their endeavour to further God's kingdom upon earth.

Placed in the heart of the city, in the midst of what will soon be the finest and prettiest spot of all, St. Andrew's Church, a massive pile of white sandstone, easily claims the first place as the finest building within the city....

The design is an easy treatment of the fourteenth century Gothic. There are three towers, the main tower raising one hundred feet above the level of the street. These towers are square for the first fifty feet, changing into the octagonal.

The main entrance to the church is on Brodie Street, and the beauty of its design cannot fail to impress even the most impartial observer.

The front entrance, Brodie Street, 2008 (Photo TLS)

Ten marble columns supporting Corinthian caps of fine carving, mark the entrance. The centre cluster of columns are capped with sculptured maple leaves to the main arch, terminating at each side with sculptured shamrocks. The other columns are capped with carvings of the thistle, the rose, the lily, and the leek, thus telling the glad welcome that awaits the people from all lands, within the sacred edifice. A wide stone entrance with a flagged floor and big Gothic doors to the right and the left give entrance into the church.

That the acme of simplicity has been attained, is the first impression the interior gives. The wide circular auditorium imparts a delightful idea of great space and light. There are four large aisles leading from the entrance, and the gallery is supported with Corinthian columns. At either side of the inside vestibule, wide, comfortable stairways lead up to the gallery and may easily be entered from the inside of the church.

All the woodwork in the interior of the building is of weathered quarterent oak; a dado of burlap, stained to match the woodwork, is the only attempt at ornamentation on the walls; from this border up to the beamed ceiling, pure white is the somewhat severe treatment.

The gallery is in the horseshoe shape, with a graceful curved railing. It is perhaps from the gallery that one gets the best effect of the whole interior. The raised seats affording a splendid view of the whole church.

There are fourteen square feet of leaded lights in the building, and the whole interior is flooded with a soft, indescribably lovely light, that pours through the stained glass windows. The most prominent window is the memorial window immediately above the choir gallery. This is the 'Good Shepherd' window and through the beauty of its colouring we read that it is dedicated "to the glory of God" presented by "Mary and Margaret" and we all know that this is the gift of the two McKellar sisters, Mrs. Deacon and Miss McKellar.

Effulgent with light, its soft glow lights up the choir gallery below. On the right side of the church and at the front, are other stained windows, one with the burning bush, the emblem of the Presbyterian faith the world over, and St. Andrew's Cross; the other with the dove of peace, and a sheaf of wheat. In all the doors are inserts of stained leaded glass, the whole effect of the rich colouring against the whiteness of the walls and ceiling, the darkness of the woodwork and furniture, making up a picture that has been the inspiration of an artist, and the admiration of all who behold it.

The choir loft is placed in the finest position, half-way between the gallery and the auditorium: it is semi-circular in form, and has accommodation for sixty members, which can be increased easily to one hundred for special occasions.

In front of the choir is the pulpit. The front gallery of the choir which makes the division between pulpit and choir, is a massive moulding of Gothic tracery, heavily panelled.

Above this on either side, raising to the roof, are the organ pipes. These pipes are of polished metal, unpainted and strikingly attractive in the decorative scheme. There are only two other churches in the

Dominion with polished organ pipes. They give forth a purer sound and are of the very best material.

The Gothic tendency to produce a richness of effect over the whole building, has been faithfully followed. There is not one jarring note in the whole picture; it is restful and beautiful, a perfect symphony of simplicity and elegance, with strength as the main idea....

The vestibules are lighted with the antique lanterns carrying out the 14th century idea....

Important in all church services is the organ, and in accordance with its other appointments, St. Andrew's organ will be a perfect one of its kind. Its cost was $5,250, Andrew Carnegie paying half the amount, the Ladies' Guild, the remainder....

This splendid edifice, completed, has cost seventy-two thousand dollars....

Who, we ask, were the men who carried out this big undertaking so well. That honour rests with the building committee and this band of faithful workers was composed of Messrs. Peter McKellar, chairman; G.R. Duncan, treasurer; David Smith, secretary; Davidson, Black, Hugh Piper, F.W. Young.

Undoubtedly, it was no easy task they carried through, and they may now rest from their labours and enjoy the result which certainly redounds to their credit. The architects, who designed, and in whose minds the perfected building existed before it became visible to our eyes, were Messrs. Stinson & Hood.

Historic Schools

The postcard reads: "Educational Institutes, Fort William, Ont., Canada", c 1910. Top row left to right: Francis Street (demolished), Isabella Street (demolished), Franklin Street (demolished): Bottom row left to right: Central Public (demolished); St. Joseph's Boarding School (demolished); Fort William Collegiate Institute (standing)

Buildings remaining: Central School Port Arthur (1884) • St. Stanislaus (1902) • St. James (1907) • Fort William Collegiate Institute (1907) • Port Arthur Collegiate Institute (1909-10) • Drew Street (1910) • Heath Park (1928) • Hillcrest Technical and Vocational Institute (1928) • Selkirk Collegiate Institute (now St. Patrick Roman Catholic High School) (1931) • Queen Elizabeth (1938)

As with its historic churches, Thunder Bay could once boast a fine collection of historic schools. But with the demolition of such venerable old schools as Prospect Street, Cornwall Avenue, Francis Street, and Franklin Street, to name a few, it makes it harder and harder to remember that time. As I was writing this chapter, Isabella Street School was being torn down to make way for a retirement home.

With the loss of these schools we are losing some of Thunder Bay's most architecturally significant buildings. For example, in losing Prospect Street School we have lost a beautiful red brick and stone building that featured a classic portico (an extended porch or colonnade) at the school's front entrance. Unique in the city, the portico supported a large sculptured metal globe and two draped figures (p. 211). In losing Cornwall Avenue School we have lost a rare Queen Anne Style building and its Simpson Island masonry (p. 214). And in losing Francis Street School we have lost another classically designed building with its magnificent Doric columns (p. 213).

The sad thing is that many of these buildings could probably have been adaptively modified to suit a number of different purposes—such as, office blocks, condominiums, apartments, etc., as I will discuss later. Even sadder, we are losing the cornerstones of our neighbourhoods. The memory-keepers of our youth. Does it matter that the places where some of your most formative memories were shaped have been bulldozed away? As I've already argued, it probably does.

In light of Thunder Bay's dismal record on maintaining and reusing historic schools, I have asked my mother, Elle Andra-Warner to reminiscence about her days attending one of the few historic schools still standing, and still functioning as a school: St. James Public School. After a 48-year absence, she recently attended her alma mater's 100th Anniversary, and found herself flooded with memories of herself as a young girl. What fun it was to remember playing alleys on the north wall or skipping in the courtyard or to meet her old kindergarten teacher. Just for a minute, time stood still, but sometimes that is all you need.

St. James Public School, c 1915 (Thunder Bay Historical Museum Society)

My Memories of St. James Public School

by Elle Andra-Warner

Historically, only a handful of Thunder Bay schools have made it to their 100th Anniversary. In 2007, the elementary school I attended as a child—the grand old St. James Public School on Court Street—joined that exclusive club. Today, it is the oldest school still operating in the city.

Originally named North Ward School, it was the second school in Port Arthur when it opened on September 3, 1907 (Central School, on Algoma Street, was the first). That same year, Port Arthur, with its population hovering around 13,000, officially became a city. To put things into perspective: Port Arthur's mayor was George Clavet; there were ten restaurants listed in the 1907 Henderson's Directory (such as the City Cafe, on Cumberland Street); and Canada's Prime Minister was Sir Wilfred Laurier.

St. James School's architectural beauty has stood the test of time. The architect, Henry Simpson of Toronto, who also designed Port Arthur Collegiate Institute and the now-demolished Cornwall Avenue School, was commissioned to build a four-roomed school out of "...solid brick, substantial, plain and at least without too much elaborate ornamentation."

Simpson designed all three schools with "...strong characteristics of the Queen Anne style, particularly in the curving Flemish gables." Art Gunnell in his article, 'This Magnificent Pile', in the Thunder Bay Historical Museum Society's *Papers & Records XXI* detailed the school's architecture:

> Segmental arched entrances outlined in white stone with oversized keystones and voussoirs, corner buttresses capped with white stone, and blocks of more white stone above and below the flat pilasters [classic columns that appear to be built in a wall] guaranteed a busy surface and called attention to the entrances. The double-hung windows of the individual classrooms were arranged in bands of four, providing almost a solid wall of glass in each classroom. With stone sills and a metal lintel above the windows, each row of windows broke up the plain wall surfaces and carried the colour scheme of the entrances around the building.

Arched entranceway of St. James Public School, 2009 (Photo EAW)

The first principal of St. James School was Miss G. Sparks. Assisting her were Miss Wink, Miss Bellman and Miss McDonald. The following year, on October 14, 1908, the *Port Arthur Daily News* reported that the average attendance in Miss Spark's Senior III and Junior III was 41 students. The article listed her 'Top Students' as Laura Churchill, Stewart Cox, Gordon McDougall and Willie Forest. In Miss Wink's Primary Grade class, average attendance was 51 students; her top students were Jack Robarts, George Marks, Vernon Bayes and Beatta Smith. The other two teachers were Miss E. Gowsell and Miss McDonald; their top students were Archie Gibbons, Hilma Nietula and Arnold Jones.

During the early 1900s, Port Arthur's population grew rapidly, and barely three years after its opening, St. James School was already too small to accommodate the increase in students. In 1910, a four-room addition was added. And then in 1914, local architects Hood and Scott were hired to add four more rooms, bringing the total number of rooms in the school to twelve. The architects had explicit instructions that their addition was to match the existing building, which required constructing the foundation walls out of Simpson Island sandstone and the entrances out of Bedford stone. In the 1970s, the gymnasium was added, a less architecturally sympathetic addition.

After a 48-year absence, I visited St. James School in 2007. Changes of course had occurred, for example, the city's first French Immersion Program started here in 1982, but the old familiar spots were still there. There were so many highlights: seeing the north wall we played 'alleys' against; walking around the open area my friends and I used to jump 'double-dutch'; and simply stepping inside the school's main floor hall, where we used to gather for assemblies, ceremonies and choir practices. Forty-eight years later, however; everything seemed so much smaller! It was good to see that the stairs, the tall doors, and the outlined entrances were still there along with the semi-circle flower bed in front. Ah yes…it still felt like 'my' St. James.

On October 25, 2007 the historic halls of St. James School

came alive with memories as it welcomed 500 alumni and former staff for its 100th Anniversary. The gym walls were lined with class pictures and stories about the long list of students who had come through its doors. Including the NHL's first Finnish-born hockey player, Albert Pudas, who played for the Toronto St. Pats/Maple Leafs; international hockey maverick, Joe Wirkkunen, who became the head coach of the Finnish National Hockey team; 1960s singer and teen idol Bobby Curtola and the popular musician/songwriter/singer Tommy Horricks, to name a few.

But the star of the 100th Anniversary—the person who received the longest standing ovation of the night—was our cherished kindergarten teacher, Miss Jean Jacobs. When the 93-year-old Miss Jacobs went up to the speaker's podium and asked how many people in the audience were her former students, the sea of hands was in the hundreds, including mine. I'll never forget Miss Jacobs. It was her patience and support that made this Estonian war refugee, who barely spoke English, feel welcome in her class. And for that I will always be grateful.

Port Arthur Collegiate Institute, c 1924. City of Thunder Bay Heritage Property. Henry Simpson, the architect of St. James School, also designed PACI in 1909. Lakehead University now owns the building. (Collection TLS)

Embodied Energy

The greenest building is the one already built.

Carl Elefante

Energy required to produce:

one brick: 14,283 BTU

one gallon of paint: 508,475 BTU

one door: 1,191,182 BTU

one barrel of cement: 1,528,126 BTU

Energy Use for Building Construction, 1976

Think of a building as a *scarce* resource. Every building that goes up is made of non-recoverable energy. This includes the energy needed to manufacture the building supplies (the bricks, lumber, paint, cement), transport the supplies (by air, ship, transport, sometimes thousands of miles), and construct the building (the labour, machines, fuel to run the machines). These elements make up the *embodied energy* of the building. Very little of this energy is recoverable.

Powter and Ross (2005) explain that "when a building is demolished, the benefits of the embodied energy (the energy invested in the building to date) are lost, and more energy is consumed in the demolition process."

The costs start to add up pretty quickly. In fact, we can calculate how wasteful it is to demolish a building by using the online calculator found at www.thegreenestbuilding.org. Very soon we find that lost embodied energy and demolition costs for, say, an average elementary school can be equivalent to wasting over a *million litres* of gasoline.

Another way to look at it, the teardown of one building can undue months of recycling work. Donovan Rypkema, the principal consultant at *PlaceEconomics*, stressed this point in a speech he gave to the *Historic Districts Council Annual Conference* in New York in 2007:

> You know we all diligently recycle our Coke cans. It's a pain in the neck, but we do it because it is good for the environment. Here is a typical building in a North American downtown—25 feet wide and 100 or 120 or 140 feet deep. Let's say that today we tear down one small building like this in your neighbourhood. We have now wiped out the entire environmental benefit from the last 1,344,000 aluminum cans that were recycled. We've not only wasted an historic building, but we've wasted months of diligent recycling by the good people of our community.

I am going to elaborate on this point a bit longer because it is so important, and, surprisingly, so little understood. Donovan Rypkema further explained that when we throw away historic buildings, we strike out three times:

> Razing historic buildings results in a triple hit on scarce resources. First, we are throwing away thousands of dollars of embodied energy. Second, we are replacing it with materials vastly more consumptive of energy. What are most historic houses built from? Brick, plaster, concrete and timber. What are among the least energy consumptive of materials? Brick, plaster, concrete and timber. What are major components of new buildings? Plastic, steel, vinyl and aluminum. What are among the most energy consumptive of materials? Plastic, steel, vinyl and aluminum. Third, reoccuring embodied energy savings increase dramatically as a building life stretches over fifty years.
>
> You're a fool or a fraud if you say you are an environmentally conscious builder and yet are throwing away historic buildings and their components.
>
> **Let me put it a different way—if you have a building that lasts 100 years, you could use 25% more energy every year and still have less lifetime energy use than a building that lasts 40 years. And a whole lot of buildings being built today won't last even 40 years.** (Bold added.)

The key is *lifetime* energy use; we tend to think of 'green' buildings as modern buildings that boast a 'green-design' or hold a LEED certificate. But we need to expand our horizons; much of the 'green-building' movement focuses on the amount of energy that a building uses *per year*, and obviously the lower the amount, the greater the praise. But, energy use per year is only one part of the equation, and in fact, the building's embodied energy—remember that is the energy that went into the manufacture and transportation of the building supplies and the construction of the building—is *15 to 30 times* greater than the amount of energy used per year. "Older buildings are a fossil fuel repository," explains Michael Jackson, chief architect with the Illinois Historic Preservation Agency, in a recent article in *Preservation* magazine. In fact, equations worked out by Jackson suggest that when embodied energy is factored in, even a new 'green-design' building will not start saving energy for 40 years. And if another building was torn down to build the new 'green-building', it will take a whopping 65 years for the energy savings to break even. It needs to be reiterated that many of these new buildings aren't even built to last that long.

This perspective shifts the balance; it isn't a case of the new, green buildings on one side, and the old, inefficient buildings on the other. Rather the older building is on the same page, if not the page before.

But what about *functional obsolescence*? What about situations where schools, churches or office blocks, no longer meet the demands of their users. The congregation gets too big and needs a new church, or the students too few and the school is forced to close.

"Functional obsolescence is real," explains Donovan Rypkema. "But for many developers, real estate owners, architects, and city officials, the response to functional obsolescence is demolition." But it doesn't have to be.

Adaptive reuse is another alternative; really, it should be the *first* alternative. In the high-cost energy world we live in, which will undoubtedly only get higher, we should feel *compelled* to find other uses for these buildings. We should constantly seek ways to minimize our wastefulness, from recycling pop cans to buildings. Especially buildings. Perhaps it helps to know that recycling buildings is not a new idea, but an old one; indeed, in 1913 Knox United Church was rolled on timber logs pulled by horses from Brodie Street to its new home on Pruden Street! If they could do it back then, we can certainly do it now.

The concept of embodied energy has to change the way we think about older buildings, although, really this is just common sense. Adaptive reuse makes more dollars and energy sense than a demolition-by-neglect or demolition-to-rebuild approach.

Royal Edward Hotel

Royal Edward Hotel, 1929 (Collection TLS)

Year Built: 1929
Architect: Dorr and Dorr, Minneapolis
Style: Art Deco
Heritage Status: City of Thunder Bay Heritage Property

"Fort William is stepping out with a dash."

Editorial on the grand opening of the Royal Edward Hotel

Fort William Daily Times Journal, April 23, 1929

Earlier I nicknamed the Royal Edward Hotel: *The Hotel That Community Pride Built And Then Forgot.* When the Royal Edward Hotel first opened its doors in 1929, it was the pride of Fort William. In fact, over 800 of its citizens became shareholders, raising $400,000 of the $500,000 needed to build the hotel (the CPR bought the rest). At the time, Fort William's population was only 25,000.

How contracted our memories have become if a hotel as heralded as the Royal Edward—I counted no less that 15 articles in the *Fort William Daily Times Journal* on opening day —could be assigned to the dustbin just 50 years later.

Where is our sense of pride, our sense of community spirit? Do we really believe progress is tearing down a perfectly good building? We have to shake ourselves out of these doldrums.

The Grand Tour 1929

I set myself a goal: what did Fort William's famous Art Deco hotel look like when it opened in 1929? It took months of searching, but I finally found my answer by pairing together the opening day reviews of the hotel published in the *Fort William Daily Times Journal* and photographs I found in an old stockholder's brochure.

Imagine the year is 1929 (just months before the big stockmarket crash), and you have just arrived from Winnipeg by train at Union Station on Syndicate Avenue. After a thirteen hour journey, you collect your luggage from the platform and hail a cab to take you to the Royal Edward Hotel. After hearing your destination, the taxi driver smiles with pride, and proceeds to tells you about the 19 foot stencilled ceilings in the ballroom, the walnut furniture in the bedrooms and the fireplace in the lounge. Soon you are at the hotel's front doors on May Street. A hotel porter promptly carries your luggage to the reception desk where the three well-dressed men pictured on page 131 are waiting to welcome you to the hotel. Your stylish surroundings leave you feeling a bit embarrassed about your wrinkled travelling clothes. The following descriptions of the hotel are from the *Fort William Daily Times Journal*, April 23, 1929:

The lobby is richly furnished with comfortable chesterfields and easy chairs with a seating capacity for 25 guests. The whole is inviting. From the lobby one enters the lounge, with its Indian rugs, a huge open fire-place adding a home-like atmosphere. It is spacious, commodious, attractive and above all, restful. Here again, the furnishings are in keeping with the luxurious standard maintained in the rest of the building.

Lobby, 1929 (Royal Edward Hotel Stockholder's Brochure)

Two spacious mezzanines front on May Street and command excellent views of the rest of the interior of the main floor. Both are adequately furnished with chesterfield chairs, card tables, writing desks and lounges. The mezzanines may be used for afternoon teas and bridge parties. Expensive rugs cover the floor.

The Lounge, off the lobby, 1929 (Royal Edward Hotel Stockholder's Brochure)

After your reservations are confirmed, a smartly dressed bellboy wearing a blue jacket and polished brass buttons, helps you carry your luggage to your room:

There are 105 bedrooms, each with bath or shower. These rooms are beautifully decorated with silk shadow cloth drapes and linen net curtains. Each room is carpeted from wall to wall with a fine quality Wilton carpet and furnished with a dresser and large mirror, writing desk, night table, easy chair, Windsor chair, bed lamps, bridge lamps and telephone.

Bedroom, 1929 (Royal Edward Hotel Stockholder's Brochure)

Sixty per cent of the rooms have twin beds. Furnishings are complete and rich. Beds are of a splendid quality. The writing table, dresser-wardrobe and Windsor chair are of walnut.

Once unpacked, you decide to explore. The elevator girl, also neatly dressed in a blue uniform with pleated skirt and forage cap, suggests you start in the stately ballroom:

Without doubt the ballroom is one of the Royal Edward's most splendid assets. It is suprisingly large, the high, vaulted ceilings increasing the sensation of bigness. Its capacity is 500 persons. Ceiling and wall electrical fixtures are rich-looking. The ballroom is going to be a very popular community centre.

The Royal Edward's ballroom has one of the finest floors in the province. It is of first grade maple, 13 by 1½ inches in width, driven up tight and well blind nailed. It is machine sanded.

The Ballroom, 1929 (Royal Edward Hotel Stockholder's Brochure)

As you walk through the building you make a mental note of the quality worksmanship:

All windows, from the second to the eighth floors are a wood double hung sash, with double glazing. Dining rooms, lobby and lounge windows have wood casements to swing out with fixed transom sash above.

All plaster used throughout the building is a wood fibre plaster with bondceret used on ceilings. The ceilings of the lobby, dining room and ballroom have no plaster. Walls in three units of the hotel are finished with a plastic paint, giving a really beautiful effect.

Ladies Parlour. 1929 (Royal Edward Hotel Stockholder's Brochure)

The exterior of the building above the second storey will be furnished with a stucco dash of a very light buff tint. It is applied with a wire brush, put on smoothly and uniformly. The interior wood finish is birch or red Philippine mahogany. Birch hand rails are installed on the staircase from the basement to the second floor. The hotel office is particularly attractive with a tiled wall on the lobby side, and cupboards and drawers opposite.

Terrazzo is carried out on an extensive scale in the lobby, part of the dining room, steps to the lounge, stairs to the mezzanines, second floor and basement, and in the toilet rooms on the first floor.

Dining Room, 1929 (Royal Edward Hotel Stockholder's Brochure)

Wrought iron work throughout is effective. There are wrought iron stair rails from the basement to the first floor and from the second floor stairs to the mezzanines. There are wrought iron drapery rods for the large windows in the dining room, lounge and balcony.

Now you understand why your taxi driver was so enthusiastic. You end your tour in the handsome restaurant and slide into one of the counter chairs and order lunch. It is packed with bankers from Victoria Avenue. There is no doubt in your mind— Fort William is the place to be!

Restaurant, 1929 (Royal Edward Hotel Stockholder's Brochure)

New Year's Dinner

JANUARY 1st, 1941

$1.00

★ ★

Celery Hearts — Assorted Olives
Grapefruit Cocktail — Tomato Juice
Cream of Fresh Tomatoes — Consomme Princess

Fried Fresh Oysters on Toast, Tartar Sauce
Broiled Filet of Lake Trout, Parsley Butter

Roast Young Turkey with Dressing, Cranberry Sauce
Broiled Filet Mignon, Fresh Mushroom Sauce
Asparagus Tips Omelette
Roast Prime Ribs of Beef au jus, Horseradish
Fried Breast of Spring Chicken with Bacon
Assorted Cold Cuts with Sweet Gherkins

Lemon Punch

French Fried, Baked, Boiled or Mashed Potatoes
Fried Sweet Potatoes
Cauliflower in Cream — Fresh Green Peas

Head Lettuce with Thousand Island Dressing

Steamed Fruit Pudding, Foamy Sauce
Pumpkin Pie — Apple Pie a la Mode
Fresh Strawberry Coupe — Fruit Brick Ice Cream
Crackers and Old Canadian or Roquefort Cheese

Assorted Fruit — After Dinner Mints

Salted Almonds

Tea — Coffee — Jersey Milk

New Year's Day Dinner Menu, Royal Edward Hotel, 1941

What people today wouldn't pay to check into an authentic Art Deco hotel, but in 1981 the hotel filed for bankruptcy and closed its doors. It owed its creditors $1.3 million dollars.

The bankruptcy trustees tried to sell the hotel to private investors, but deal after deal fell through. Finally, the trustees held a firesale of the hotel's removable goods and a long line of people waited to bid on its silver wagon service, towels, glasses, coffee urns, tea service, candle holders, juice squeezers, china—some of it enscribed: "Paragon, Fine China, Manufactured to HM Queen Elizabeth, The Queen Mother, Made in England"; and less glamorous items such as the hotel's toilets and urinals.

Still, nobody wanted to buy the hotel; so the City decided to buy it for $145,000 and tear it down.

"I don't think anybody can make a case that the building has any use," stated Councillor Dick Waddington to the *Chronicle Journal*, November 11, 1981.

However, in 1984 the building was still standing and the Thunder Bay Non-Profit Housing Corporation pitched a proposal to city hall to convert the hotel into a 64-unit subsidized apartment building. But they were turned down.

It looked like the way was finally clear to tear down the hotel; but for a strike by 375 City workers.

This gave the determined housing corporation more time to muster its forces. And support was growing.

"It just makes no sense to have a vacant lot when for the same money you can have housing," Councillor Dale Willoughby was quoted as saying in the *Chronicle Journal.*

Mayor Walter Assef and Councillor Sterling Lysnes even gave the media a tour of the hotel to show that it was worth saving.

"The rooms are absolutely very encouraging," Mayor Assef was quoted in the *Chronicle Journal* (Jan 4, 1984). "The rugs are beautiful, everything is beautiful, the toilets are beautiful."

Finally, in the fall of 1984 City Council voted 7-6 to spare the hotel the wrecking ball. And a couple of months later the

Thunder Bay Non-Profit Housing Corporation secured the funding it needed to convert the historic hotel into much needed subsidized apartments.

One last interesting 'nugget'. In the course of doing the research for this book, I came across an intriguing story in the *Lakehead Living* (1981) that mentioned the hotel's initials—'RE'—had once been embedded in silver in the lobby's terrazzo floor. Although I couldn't confirm it, the article also mentioned that the initials were inlaid with some of the last silver mined from Silver Islet. Apparently, the initials had long been covered up by a rug, so most guests would never have known they were there. I have to shake my head: if you were a guest of the hotel wouldn't you have found that Art Deco flourish with its potential connection to one of the world's richest silver mines worthy of display?

So, decades later and after many renovations: did the initials still exist? I went to the Royal Edward to find out. After explaining my dilemma to the staff, it didn't take long to solve the mystery. In a little room off the reception area—there on the floor were the initials! I felt such a surge of joy rush through me, history felt alive to me; I swear I could picture myself waltzing across the Royal Edward's maple ballroom.

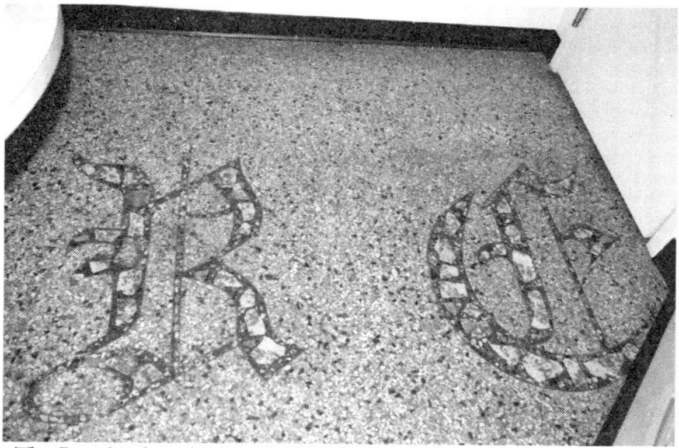

The Royal Edward initials embedded with silver, 2008 (Photo TLS)

Although I would much rather be checking into the Royal Edward Hotel as it looked *circa* 1929; if it had to go, I am at least glad it was not torn down.

Not only is the hotel a significant architectural landmark in the city and a monument to community pride, it was also *energetically* expensive to build and would have been extremely wasteful to tear down.

If the Royal Edward had been torn down all of the initial effort and resources that went into building the hotel would have literally evaporated into thin air; in addition, the demolition debris would have added a significant burden to Thunder Bay's landfill sites. It would have been ridiculously wasteful to tear down a perfectly good building, rather than put it to good use.

As I mentioned earlier, we can calculate how wasteful a teardown would have been. The eight remaining storeys of the Royal Edward Hotel encompass approximately 91,000 sq. feet. If these eight storeys had been torn down (some of the hotel was), the loss of embodied energy would have been equivalent to 102,830,000 MBTU. But that is not all, we also have to factor in the costs associated with demolishing the Royal Edward Hotel, which would have added another 1,092,000,000 BTU of lost energy.

These are very large impressive numbers, but they are hard to appreciate on their own, so let's convert the potential lost energy to the equivalent litres of gasoline.

If the Royal Edward had been torn down, the loss of embodied energy and costs associated with the demolition would have been equivalent to dumping 3,420,763 litres of gasoline down the drain. I repeat: 3,420,763 litres.

This should give us pause for thought—in the high-cost energy world we live in today, tearing down any building, historic or otherwise, should be a last resort.

Banking District: Victoria Avenue

≈

Canadian Bank of Commerce
Traders Block (Amethyst Gift Centre)
Royal Bank
Bank of Montreal (Ukrainian Credit Union & Victoria Ave)
Pattenick (Roy) Building
& The Thunder Bay Museum, Donald Street

Canadian Bank of Commerce, Victoria Avenue, 2003 (Photo TLS)

Built: 1911
Architect: B.D. Horsburgh
Style: Classical Revival
Heritage Status: City of Thunder Bay Heritage Property

When I walk down Victoria Avenue, I see such potential. I imagine cafes and bookstores and crowds of people. Shoppers are enjoying their day, not in a mall, but walking along one of the most historic and architecturally significant streets of Thunder Bay. This is the section of Victoria Avenue from May Street to Simpson Street.

This section of Victoria Avenue is the historic 'Banking District' of Fort William. At different times the street has been home to The Traders Bank; The Bank of Montreal; The Royal Bank; The Canadian Bank of Commerce; The Ray, Street and Company Bank; The Toronto Dominion Bank; The Commercial Bank of Manitoba; and The Merchants Bank of Canada.

The whole block is a history lesson writ large: a visual reminder of Fort William's heady early days when grain, timber, silver and the railway were king.

But on my imaginary shopping trip, I am more concerned with meeting my friends for a green tea, let's say at a cafe in the historic Pattenick building, where we sit admiring the tin ceilings and grand staircase, and then stroll along the street browsing in the big windows of the historic storefronts. We wander into locally-owned shops and artisans' studios; one-of-a-kind businesses that you can only find in this area of town. The vibe is similar to walking down a street in Old Montreal or Stephen Avenue in Calgary or the Forks in Winnipeg.

Although we don't know it, we are also helping out the local economy. A study done of Chicago businesses found that for every $100 consumers spent at a local business, $68 remained in the local economy (www.AndersonvilleStudy.com). In comparison, for every $100 consumers spent at a chain store, only $43 stayed in the local economy. Furthermore, for every square foot of space occupied by a local business, the local economic impact is $179 versus $105 for a chain store. The great architecture is thrown in for free.

I definitely have a soft spot for Victoria Avenue, mainly because it is home to my favourite building in the city: the

Canadian Bank of Commerce. In fact, it is because of this building that I decided to write this book.

More specifically, it was a fire at the bank on February 10, 2007 that got my attention. The fire broke out on the third floor of the bank and quickly spread to its lower floors. Very soon almost 100 years of history was going up in smoke. No one was injured, but the building was considered a write-off and was soon scheduled for demolition.

Despite many Letters to the Editor written by concerned citizens, several editorials, television and radio coverage, an online petition that received hundreds of signatures in its first few days, and the fact that the Canadian Bank of Commerce was one of only 26 Designated Heritage Buildings in the city, City Council decided to demolish the bank.

Fortunately, there are people in this city who do see the potential of this building and this street, one of them being a local architect named Mr. Ahsanul Habib. Mr. Habib saved the bank days before it was scheduled for demolition. At his own risk, he purchased the bank from the previous owner, paid for the demolition costs of the bank's interior and salvaged the bank's classic facade.

When I asked Mr. Habib why he did it, he simply said he knew he had to save the bank from being demolished—that it was worth something.

He explained: "Buildings have cultural ties, we have relationships with buildings even if they are not architectural masterpieces. If we lose those buildings, we lose those ties."

Moreover, Mr. Habib explained: "There is a green aspect to preserving a building, you have to consider the labour, the material costs, and the pollution that go into producing one brick. Think of all of the energy it costs to produce and transport a brick from Southern Ontario to Thunder Bay. By saving and reusing old buildings, even newer box-stores that are already built, we save money."

He added: "We can't save all old buildings, but when we can, we should."

And Mr. Habib has. Not only has he saved the Canadian Bank of Commerce and the Pattenick (Roy) building across the street, he has also saved another architectural masterpiece in the city, the Fort William Collegiate Institute which will become condominiums.

Mr. Habib has also saved buildings that are not architectural masterpieces; such as the Capitol Theatre on Victoria Avenue which he has donated to a local non-profit arts group to be turned into a performing arts centre; the Gerry Building on Victoria Avenue; the Montreal Warehouse on the Kam River which is now used for storage, although one day it may be turned into a bustling marketplace, which was his original idea; and he has converted Riverdale School into condominiums. Rather than ending up in a landfill, these buildings have a new lease on life (and generate more tax-revenue), and we, as a city, are the better for it.

Victoria Avenue, c 1920. The Canadian Bank of Commerce is on the right; the Roy Building (Pattenick's; built in 1908) is directly across from it. Many of the buildings seen in this postcard are still standing. (Collection TLS)

Sometimes we get stuck seeing a familiar place in one way, and forget there are a hundred other ways to see it. That is what has happened to Victoria Avenue, but it doesn't have to be. We need to peel back some of Victoria Avenue's layers, to see the diamond, and not the rough, again. To tell stories about the days when it was a bustling street in the heart of Fort William's downtown (if in doubt, reread the chapter on the *Royal Edward Hotel*).

Every city needs a good downtown. (Thunder Bay could have two: Victoria Avenue and Cumberland Street/Court Street/ Red River Road). Downtowns 'centre' people. "Downtown has traditionally been the focal point for community sense of place...The downtown, usually the oldest part of a city, is a unique combination of forms and structures from various eras and has been the setting for major events of the past. It is a place that cannot be replicated by new shopping centres and neighbourhoods, no matter how architecturally exciting they may be," writes Larry R. Ford in *Growth and Change* (1974).

In other words, a city's downtown reflects its soul. And people do indeed judge a city by the state of its downtown. We need to ask ourselves, what does it say about Thunder Bay that its downtown has been allowed to slide into neglect?

The good news is that we already have the buildings, let's use them to their full potential. This is what I see when I walk down Victoria Avenue.

The Morning Herald, Fort William, April 12, 1911

BANK OF COMMERCE A VERY HANDSOME BUILDING

Temporary Framework Torn Away Last Night Shows Latest Addition to Victoria Ave Business Structures

The temporary framework at the front of the new Bank of Commerce on Victoria Avenue was torn down last night, and an unobstructed view of the building may be obtained for the first time.

The details of design in the edifice follow classic lines, and the general feeling is keeping with the purposes for which the building is intended. The building throughout is constructed with the best modern practice, and will distinctly enhance the appearance of Victoria Avenue.

The facade, which consists of light grey terra-cotta, consists of an order of Doric columns, running through two storeys and surrounded by an emtablature pierced by windows, and a parallel parapet. The window sashes and frames resemble solid bronze, and the front is also ornamented by a copper cornice.

The entire main floor will be occupied by the bank, and will contain the banking hall and manager's room. The banking hall is a large room, thirty-seven feet long and thirty-five feet wide, and is ornamented by fluted plaster columns with a deep enriched cornice and ornamental ceiling.

The manager's room and vestibule also have an ornamental cornice and ceiling, while the walls are laid out in moulded panels.

The fixtures of the bank are of Honduras mahogany. The space in the office will be large enough to accommodate three tellers' cages.

The second floor will be devoted to suites of modern office apartments, while the top is arranged to provide accommodation for the members of the banking staff, for whose use a large sitting room has been provided on the top floor.

Architect's drawing of the Canadian Bank of Commerce, 1911. *The Morning Herald.*

The building is heated throughout by hot water and the walls are tinted in pleasing soft tones.

The new structure has been designed by B.D. Horsburgh, A.R.I.B.A., supervising architect of the Dominion Realty Company, Ltd., of Toronto, who are erecting the building, and for whom Mr. Robert Alford is acting as local works superintendent. Messrs. Seaman and Penniman, of Fort William and Port Arthur, are the general contractors.

I couldn't resist the next article. What would a Banking District be without a few robberies? A few months after the Canadian Bank of Commerce opened, the Royal Bank down the street was the scene of a brazen bank hold-up. The local newspapers reported it was one of the most spectacular bank robberies ever seen in Western Canada.

The Port Arthur Daily News, October 23, 1911

EX EMPLOYEE OF BANK HOLDS UP TELLER AND GETS AWAY WITH $5,000

Sensational Robbery of Fort William Institution During Noon Hour—Thief Arrested and Money Found in Room

Levelling a revolver at Teller H.L. Dickson, of the Royal Bank Fort William, and covering him with the weapon while he gathered bills from the counter, A.R. Running this noon made a getaway with nearly $5,000 in his possession, to be afterwards arrested without any of the stolen property on his person.

The robbery was committed during the lull of the business in the noon hour when no other employee besides Dickson was in the bank and was the boldest thing ever pulled off in either of the two cities. The alleged thief was formerly an employee of the bank.

Surprised The Teller

It was about 12:45 when Running entered the bank. Having been formerly engaged in the bank and having left a trunk in the building on his connections with the institution being severed he was quite familiar to the teller on duty, Mr. Dickson, and the latter paid no attention to him as he proceeded to the rear of the building ostensibly for the purpose of getting something from his trunk.

Evidently Running watched for a good opportunity and at a moment when the door of the teller's cage was open, suddenly flashed his revolver on Mr. Dickson with the demand:

"Up with your hands!"

Mr. Dickson did not believe the man was serious in his intentions and replied:

"What's the matter with you? Are you crazy?"

"No, I am not crazy. This is a real holdup and I mean every word of it."

Gathering Up The Cash

Mr. Dickson was taken so completely by surprise that he had no opportunity to save the cash from the designs of his former fellow-employee and could merely do as he was told as he looked into the muzzle of a gun behind which were a pair of eyes which flashed with a sort of insane anger that left no doubt as to the intentions of the man.

All he could do was to stand helplessly by and watch Running gather up the bills from the counter until he had taken all in sight, estimated at a sum exceeding $5,000.

That done Running ordered his victim to leave the building by way of the front door. Dickson did this and Running followed him into the street.

In Pursuit

Running then made a dash along Victoria Avenue in the direction of the Coal Docks [East End]. The alarm was quickly passed to the people on the street and a general pursuit followed in which most of the city police force soon joined.

A clerk of the Bank of Ottawa named Harkness was entering the Royal Bank just as the robber and the teller were leaving and he corroborated the description given of the fleeing man.

The fact that Running was well known also helped in his pursuit, but he evaded the arms of the law for nearly three-quarters of an hour, when he was found calmly sitting in a chair at the Pacific Hotel; where he had been boarding for some time, and was placed under arrest by Sergeant Watkins.

When searched after the arrest, Running did not have any of the money he was alleged to have stolen in his possession

Found The Money

After taking the prisoner to the cells, Sergeant Watkins went to his rooms at 228 Brodie Street and there made a search in which he was successful, finding the bills stowed away in a suitcase.

The amount found was $4,835, which, the manager of the bank says, is all that disappeared.

Running will appear before the magistrate for his preliminary hearing tomorrow morning.

The prisoner was, up to a few weeks ago, employed with the Royal Bank, but on September 21 was discharged for reason. He had formerly been with branches of the same bank in Winnipeg and in Brockville, where his home is. He is 24 years of age and was engaged to be married next Thursday.

When taken to the police station, Running made no statement whatever.

So what happened to Running? The local newspapers were quick to label him a "mad man"; the doctor who examined him stated that he was in a "very wrought up condition." Even his fiancee offered that his "mental machinery has slipped a cog." In the end, the Royal Bank decided not to press charges "due to the peculiar features of the case"; however, the bank did announce they would no longer leave one teller alone to transact business over the lunch hour.

At the time of the robbery, the city of Fort William was in the process of building a police station just around the corner from Victoria Avenue on Donald Street. The stated reason for the location: "It is a short half block from the present city hall and one block removed from the block in which a big percentage of the arrests are made. Prisoners can be brought through the lanes to cell rooms and arrests will attract little or no public attention" (*Fort William Daily Times Journal*, July 15, 1910).

When the building opened in 1912, it was hailed as one of the finest police stations on the continent. The article below, announcing its opening, is a lovely reminder of how times have changed; probably no other elevator in the city has been written about in such glowing terms!

Today, the police station is the Thunder Bay Museum, another great example of how a historic building can be recycled.

Fort William Daily Times Journal, July 22, 1912

POLICE ARE MOVING INTO THEIR NEW $80,000 HOME ON DONALD STREET

Prisoners Are Being Put in Cells and Police Court Will Convene There Tomorrow—Has 'Real Live' Elevator

The Fort William police department is today moving into the new police station and court house building recently erected at a cost of $80,000 on Donald Street. The police court will be conducted in the new court room tomorrow morning at the usual hour. In connection with the police court sessions several innovations are scheduled to be put into effect. The sessions are to be a source of entertainment to persons otherwise unemployed. If the crowd of spectators assumes uncomfortable proportions it is probable that an

officer will be placed on the door and only persons directly interested in pending cases admitted.

Is Police Workshop

Up to the present time police court sessions here have been of a slightly informal nature, owing largely to the inadequate arrangements, but it is expected that several changes will be the order of the day in the new building, which is a police workshop proper. As in practically every court, persons in the court room awaiting the opening of the session will be expected to rise and stand when the magistrate enters and remain standing until he takes his seat on the bench.

It is expected that much of the furniture will be installed in the new building this afternoon. In any event all offenders arrested today and this evening will be incarcerated in the new building.

The public have read so much about the new building that the only thing which will add to their information concerning it is a personal visit. It is not unlikely that an "At Home" announcement will be made soon in order that the public may inspect the building without the unpleasant necessity of any official business.

Finest On Continent

As is generally known, the building is perhaps the finest on the continent used by the police department of a city anything like the population of Fort William.

Aside from the fact that it is needed it will be a perpetual advertising asset. There is one feature of the building which, while perhaps the most interesting, has been only slightly mentioned. This feature is the elevator, and it is 'some feature'.

It is an automatic electric elevator and in this case automatic means automatic. The elevator does itself 'pracomatic'. This elevator does of itself practically everything that an elevator boy does except talk, sleep and eat, and it does it without delay.

All users of the elevator have to do is to push buttons, and by pushing them the elevator can be made to do everything that an elevator boy can make any ordinary elevator do, except drop.

For instance, if you are on the top floor and want to ride down, you go to the elevator landing and push a button. If the door of the landing where the elevator chances to be is closed, the elevator will respond by coming up and stopping at the third floor landing.

As soon as the elevator stops at your landing you can open the door, which you could not open before.

You cannot start it down until you close the door, but as soon as you leave the landing safe you push the button indicating the floor you desire to go to and down, or up, you go to that identical floor. However, you may have made a mistake in thinking of the floor you wanted to go to and have recalled the correct floor after touching the indicator.

It's Very Simple

All you have to do is push another button and all previous 'pushes' do not count. You make another start for any floor, on to your destination, or back to the landing from which you started.

There is not another elevator in the land which has anything on the elevator in the new Fort William police building and it will in all probability be some time before any improvements are suggested. About everything ever thought of in connection with electrical equipment is there and William Hauto, the caretaker of the building, says he has a suspicion that it is alive.

The Thunder Bay Museum, the former Police Station, 2008. City of Thunder Bay Heritage Property (Photo TLS)

Pleasant Surprises

When I was compiling the buildings I wanted to include in this book, I decided not to limit myself only to Thunder Bay's well-known, architecturally significant buildings. I also wanted to include vernacular or commonplace buildings, because, really, all buildings have a story to tell. And most of us live and work in relatively commonplace buildings, never pausing to think about the: 'What happened here?' stories embedded in the bricks and mortar. The buildings in this section should give you pause for thought, and may change the way you look at even the most mundane buildings in the city.

Abdou Block

The Abdou Block, corner of Chrsitie and McLaughlin Streets, 2007 (Photo TLS)

Year Built: 1907
Architect: Unknown
Style: Vernacular
Heritage Status: None

Where in the world is the Abdou Block, you are probably wondering? Even if I told you it is located at the corner of Christie and McLaughlin Streets in the East End, you probably still would not be able to picture it. Of all of the buildings included in this book, this one will undoubtedly be the least known. Which is good, that is exactly what I was hoping for.

In my many hours of microfilm work at the Brodie Street Library, I would come across some pretty unusual newspaper stories. On any given day, I might read a detailed description of the beautiful gowns worn by society ladies at the Mariaggi's *Bal Poudre* or the gory details of a suicide at a local hotel.

I also came across the following newspaper article written by a local reporter in 1908. One January afternoon, the anonymous reporter and his friend decided to walk to the East End and talk to a few of its shopkeepers about the state of their business. As an anthropologist, I realized this was a fascinating, albeit probably overly rosy, glimpse into the working-class world of the Coal Docks.

Finding this article was like digging up a long-forgotten time capsule. It presents such a *hopeful* vision of the East End: imagine a time when the East End was home to over 25 businesses and its real estate was considered a good investment.

I will meet up with you at the end of the article, to tell you about the follow-up research I did on this story.

Fort William Daily Times Journal, January 19, 1908

GREATH GROWTH OF COAL DOCK

That Section of the City Now Has Over Four Thousand Inhabitants and Twenty-Five Stores

While walking along the lower end of Simpson Street one afternoon lately, in a reminiscent mood, the writer

who, by the way, has been a resident of Fort William for a number of years, was accosted by an old friend's voice.

"Hello, old fellow, what are you thinking about?"

"I was just thinking of the changes in the appearance of this section of our city in the last few years, and how wonderfully this end seems to have been built up."

"I have often thought of that myself. What do you say to taking a walk through the Coal Dock section till we see what changes really have taken place?'

"Very well," I said. "I have the whole afternoon free and am willing."

My friend stated that he had several friends who started into business there some years ago, and others who had started by recently. These we decided to call upon. We first went to see his friend, Mr. Nisby, who, within the past year, had opened a dry goods store on the lower end of Simpson Street.

On inquiring how business was going, Mr. Nisby led us to believe that it was good considering the time of the year, and that he was well satisfied with his venture.

"A number of my countrymen on the other side of the tracks who are in business, also report the same," he told us.

After a few minutes more conversation we resumed our walk on to McTavish Street, from where we obtained a view of many buildings of comparatively recent erection, the majority of which are of a very fair class. While commenting on this fact, we reached the corner of Christie and McLaughlin Streets, where we were confronted by a splendid new brick block, erected last year by Peter Abdou.

Entering the store we found Mr. Abdou waiting on a number of customers. Till he was at leisure, we conversed about the increase in population, which warrant the building of such a block.

Mr. Abdou soon joined us and we fell to talking of old times. Complimented on his new block, the owner remarked:

"Yes, but it has been a paying investment. Some five years ago, I thought I saw good business possibilities in this section, and I started a small general store, the first one to be started in this neighbourhood.

"From that time on my business has been constantly increasing. I moved the building I opened up in, and last year erected this block on the corner, and I am well pleased with my action."

Immediately adjoining Mr. Abdou's new building we found the branch bank of Ray, Street & Co., with R.H. Neeland as manager. Here we found Mr. Neeland comfortably located and fully equipped to look after the banking and insurance business of this locality.

We left with the idea that the starting of this branch would no doubt prove of great convenience to the residents.

After a half-hour's walk along the different streets, we called upon another old-timer, J.M. Pallack, who for the past four years has conducted a general store on the corner of McIntosh and McIntyre Streets.

It took but a few minutes to get Mr. Pallack interested in talking of the changes that have taken place to the vicinity since he first started his store.

"I think," said he, "that I can claim to be one of the old residents of Fort William. I have been here nearly twenty years."

We knew that Mr. Pallack had been employed by the John King Co., Snelgrove Bros., and several other business houses, so we felt we were in the company with one who would appreciate with us the improved conditions.

During the conversation, which followed, Mr. Pallack spun a story the facts of which possibly many of our residents do not know. He started to talk of conditions as they were when he first opened his store about five years ago.

"You know," he said, "five or six years ago, land down in this section could be bought very cheap. Some men held whole blocks of real estate, and you could get a lot very cheap.

"I thought I saw a good investment and I purchased a number. Four years ago I decided to enter business for myself, and I have been glad I did ever since."

"The land values have increased wonderfully these last few years. This I attribute chiefly to the increase of population, owing to the demand for men for the enlarged C.P.R. works.

"Also I think it can be attributed to the betterment of conditions. When I first started here, the only available water supply was from the river, where one had to go with pails and barrels. The town authority put in a hydrant, where they believed the greatest number would be benefited, and I was commissioned to look after it.

"I used to get the handsome salary of 20 per cent for attending to it. Now we have mains laid in a number of streets and we hope in the coming year to see these farther extended.

"I believe a good movement is on foot to prosecute vigorously more sewer facilities. We now have a good sewer system on McTavish Street from the C.P.R freight sheds to the broom factory, on Christie to McLaughlin, then to McIntosh and the river. I think an outlet will be made on McLeod in the near future.

"When we get our good sewer and water connections we will be in still better shape."

Speaking on the generally improved appearance of the section, Mr. Pallack continued:

"You remember a few years ago, the majority of the buildings down here were tar-papered shacks. Now there are few of these. As the residents, most of who are from the eastern countries across the ocean, began to get a little money saved ahead, they began to improve their homes.

"Although a number of shacks still remain, the desire seems to be to build much better houses."

During our talk we spoke of the number of small stores, all of which seemed to be doing a fair amount of business. A near guess was given that there are now about 28 stores in the Coal Dock section. These comprise dry goods, gents' furnishings, jewellery, bakery, laundries, grocery stores and a dairy.

During our walk we could not help believing that the statements made by Mr. Pallack were correct. We remembered well that in the past only three or four stores were to be seen, where now there appears to be about 25 or 30.

Another feature that impressed us was the numerous improvements that have been made by the C.P.R., the Imperial Oil Co., and the Empire Elevator Co. It seems only a short time ago when we used to go down to the docks as far as the old range lighthouse, and from there be able to look out over the bay. Now this is an impossibility.

A vast change has taken place. The view from this point is now completely shut out by the enlargement of the C.P.R. coal handling point, the Imperial Oil Co.'s buildings, and the fine large grain house of the Empire Elevator Co.

Retracing our steps at length homewards, we noticed the ruins of the new Catholic church, which was recently burned.

Our thoughts turned to the question, "Will the church be rebuilt?"

On inquiry, we were told that it is the intention to rebuild the edifice in the near future. In the meantime, services are being held daily in the building owned by Mr. Abdou, with Father Maynard as officiating priest who devotes his whole time to the welfare of the residents.

Besides this church there is also a Lutheran church and the Baptist mission, both doing good work among their people.

The Catholic church was rebuilt on McIntosh St. as St. Peter's Slovak Church in 1911. (Photo TLS 2007)

While this section is generally termed the 'Italian Colony' or 'Little Italy' by a trip through one is impressed with the large number of nationalities that are really represented. These include Italians, Syrians,

Pollocks, Greeks, Russians, Slavs, Hungarians, Galicians, Finnlanders, Frenchmen, Englishmen, and even Chinamen.

After having spent most of the afternoon in seeing the growth of our Coal Dock district, we decided to call at the city assessor's office with an endeavour to find out how our impressions of the actual growth agreed with figures he would be able to give us.

We inquired of the population of the district some five or six years ago, as well as the total assessed value. This information was readily given, the figures proving even a greater surprise than we had anticipated.

Here we found that about five or six years ago, the estimated populace of the coal dock section was between 750 and 800 people, with the total assessed value of the land to be about $57,500.

Since that time the population has been increased, until now the number is between 3,000 and 3,500 inhabitants.

The assessed value, owing to the many improvements in buildings, etc., has also made a remarkable jump, the figure reaching to the total of nearly $225,000.

On parting with my friend, I thanked him for his suggestion of the trip feeling assured that I had spent a profitable afternoon.

My curiousity was piqued: could Mr. Abdou's store still be standing? And if it was, what kind of shape could it possibly be in? After reading the article, I decided to drive to the East End to find out.

As I drove over the East End bridge, I noticed my heart was beating a little faster. Although I had prepared myself to find a vacant lot, I held out hope that the building might still be standing— waiting for me to find it 99 years later.

I turned onto Christie Street and then stopped at the intersection with McLaughlin. I immediately noticed two large buildings on the south-east and south-west corners of the intersection.

Was one of them Mr. Abdou's?

One building was a large white building with a fire hydrant in front of it on the east side of the street and the other a large cream-coloured building on the west side.

I parked the car and took a couple of pictures of the cream-coloured building; it looked more likely to have been around in Mr. Abdou's time. The other building was a white building with a stucco facade and concrete blocks; I guessed it had been built in the 1950s. I didn't see any indication of the Abdou name on either building.

So, how to figure out which building was the real Abdou Block? Or perhaps neither were.

To try to sort it out, I headed to the Thunder Bay Archives. My friend Dawn Kannegiesser-Mitchell and her 6-month-old son, Campbell, volunteered to help.

We spread ourselves out on the big tables in the lobby of the Archives and started going through the city's Henderson Directories. The Henderson Directories are a precursor of the Yellow Pages; they list the phone numbers and addresses of individuals and businesses in a city. We started with the 1907 directory and it didn't take long to find the Abdou name; in fact, Peter Abdou was the first name in the directory. He was listed as a grocer, and he and his wife, Sarah, were listed as living at

538 McLaughlin. I was more than a little relieved to find out that Peter Abdou really did exist!

In the business section of the Henderson Directory, we also found the Abdou 'General Store' listed at 538 McLaughlin. Things were coming together. But now we had to determine if 538 McLaughlin was actually at the intersection with Christie Street, and whether it was on the east or west side of the street.

To figure out this next piece of the puzzle we needed to locate 538 McLaughlin on the 1914 City Fire Insurance Map. The Fire Insurance Map provides a bird's-eye view of buildings in the city and information on their construction materials.

Wearing protective white gloves, we pinpointed 538 McLaughlin on the map. It was on the south-east corner of Christie and McLaughlin. The map even listed the building at 538 McLaughlin as being made of concrete blocks and having a fire hydrant in front of it, just as I had observed on the ground. But I still wasn't convinced: what if a newer building had been erected in its place over the last 99 years?

To be sure I had the right building, I had to do some more investigative work. Putting together pieces of information provided by Matt Szybalski of the Thunder Bay Archives, indicating that the City Fire Insurance Maps show no change in the building's construction from 1914 to 1951, and information from Lorna Veal of the City's Planning Division, that confirmed no demolition or major construction permits were taken out on this property (permits were taken out to alter the facade and interior over the last 50 years), assured me that this is Peter Abdou's original building.

It also confirmed that I had taken a picture of the wrong building—Mr. Abdou's store was indeed the building that I had judged too modern to be 99 years old. Suddenly, this nondescript, nothing-special building had become a lot more special.

Armed with this last piece of the puzzle, we got back in the car and drove to the East End. This time I took pictures of Mr. Abdou's building, pictured on page 160. Although its last proprietor has closed up shop, the building is still in remarkably good shape.

After I took the picture, I paused to imagine Mr. Abdou standing on the front doorway, leaning on his broom, answering the newspaper reporter's questions. He could never have imagined that his spontaneous interview would have led us on a wild goose chase almost 100 years later.

But I was not done yet. Now I wanted to know who were the Abdous?

"Who Was Involved?"

I assumed my search would come to a dead end rather quickly. There are no Abdous lisited in the current Thunder Bay phonebook and I did not think a general merchant in the East End in the early 1900s would have left much of a historical footprint. But I am glad to say, I was mistaken.

I have Mark Chochla of the Thunder Bay Historical Museum Society to thank for putting me in touch with several useful leads, including his own article on the Abdous published in the *Chronicle Journal*, a 1966 *Times Journal* article, and the 1901 and 1911 Canada Census. Independently of me, Mark had also conducted research on the Abdous. Who would have thought!

So this is what we know:

The first record we have of the Abdous is the 1901 Canada Census which lists the family living in Toronto. We know that they came to Canada from Syria in 1898.

Peter (1866-1938) and Sarah (also spelt Sola or Salha; 1868-1921) had seven children, two of whom were born in Canada and five in Syria. The names of the five boys are: Caeser (also spelt Aiser, Iser, or Luishora); Charles (Calele); Michael; Thomas (Antonia); and Ted (Theophile or Toufic). The names of the two girls are Sultana and Silena (Sally).

By 1902, the family had moved to the East End of Fort William and opened up the first general store in the area, and by

1907 Peter had built the store at the corner of Christie and McLaughlin.

In the 1909 Henderson Directory, three sons are listed as living with their parents; Caeser is listed as a manager, Charles as a clerk, and Michael as a bookkeeper.

In 1911, the boys had changed jobs: Caeser who is 28 years old is now a painter living at 735 Simpson Street; Charles who is 24 is a sign writer still living at home; and Michael who is 21 is an employee at the Empire City Grocery (located at 125 ½ May St S).

The Empire City Grocery was owned by his mother, Sarah. Peter is listed as being retired; he was 48 years old.

The Abdous were hard workers. In the 1911 Census, the boys reported they worked 65 hours/ week, making $720/ year. Not a bad wage considering a feature film at the Gaiety Theatre on Cumberland Street was only 10 cents in 1911; a dozen eggs were 35 cents at the Brown Meet Co. on May St; and a two-piece suit at McNulty's in Port Arthur was on sale for $10.

The Census also records that all of the children could read and write English, and that English and 'Syrian' (Lebanese) were commonly spoken at home.

The Abdous' hard work paid off. By my count they owned at least four businesses in the city: the General Store on McLaughlin St.; The Empire City on May St.; The Economy Store on Simpson St.; and a pool hall on Simpson St.

The Economy Store (640 Simpson St.) was a clothing store owned by Caeser. Around 1914, his younger brother, Charles, acquired the building next to Caeser at 642 Simpson Street and became the proprietor of a pool hall.

I was curious to know what had become of the property at 640-642 Simpson Street. Once again, I predicted the most likely scenario, a vacant lot or a boarded-up building.

But, I should know better by now. You will never guess what this former pool hall has turned into—and that it is still a thriving business. Keep reading, it was such a pleasant surprise I decided the building needed its own chapter.

Back to the Abdous. In 1913, Peter decided to take his two youngest children, Ted and Sally, to visit his hometown in Syria (later to become part of Lebanon). Unfortunately World War I started just after they arrived and the family became stuck in Syria during the fighting. Ted, who wasn't yet a teenager, became a translator for the British army. His brother Michael also served in the war, enlisting with the 52nd Battalion of Port Arthur.

Peter never did get back to Canada, he died in Lebanon in 1938 and never saw his wife again, she died in Fort William in 1921. Ted and Sally didn't return to Fort William until 1924, but by then job prospects in the city were poor, so they migrated to the United States. Three brothers also migrated to Southern Ontario and the United States. Only Caeser and Sultana stayed in Fort William.

To round out our picture of the Abdous, we need one more piece of information: you might be wondering why Peter Abdou allowed Father Maynard to hold church services in his store after St. Peter's burnt down. That seems like a generous offer from a Muslim family.

But that is assuming the Abdous were Muslim; in fact, the 1911 Census records their religion as Roman Catholic. I was also able to track down Michael's WWI enlistment form, which records his birthplace as Hasroun, Syria (later Lebanon). Hasroun is an ancient Roman Catholic village about 105 miles north of Beirut in the mountainous region of Lebanon.

That explains why a Syrian family allowed a French-Canadian priest to hold Roman Catholic services in their store. It also speaks volumes about the strong community ties in the East End: Father Maynard's congregation included not only Syrians, but members of the Slovak, Polish, Ukrainian, French, English and Italian communities.

I am amazed that a random building in the East End led me down such a historically rich path. It makes me wonder about all of the other stories that are out there waiting to be told.

Furniture Recycle & Hardisty Street: The Warehouse District

Furniture Recycle (left) and warehouses along Hardisty Street, 2009 (Photo EAW)

Year Built: c. 1905
Architect: Unknown
Style: Vernacular
Heritage Status: None

Hardisty Street, which runs between Simpson Street and the railway tracks in Fort William, encompasses the 'Warehouse District' of Thunder Bay. The prevalence of brick warehouses and sturdy storage buildings gives the street a more industrial feel than other areas of the city. Driving down Hardisty Street is like driving back in time; yes it is gritty, but its grittiness is a monument to the hard work that was required to build the city. Thunder Bay wasn't built out of sugar.

At the turn of the century, Hardisty Street was one of the most well-travelled areas of the city, as freight and people were constantly coming and going, which today makes it one of the most interesting and historical sections of town.

My introduction to Hardisty Street was made through the second-hand furniture store *Furniture Recycle.* On my first visit to the store, which I thought was going to be a normal, uneventful shopping trip, I was thrown a loop. This place is an architectural showpiece. As soon as you open the door, you are faced with a dilemma. Where was one supposed to look first—up at the 16' exposed Douglas fir beams holding up the 11' ceiling, or down at the never-ending hardwood floor?

My head was on a swivel, something I am sure the owner, Gilles Mondoux, is used to by now. I walked around the massive showroom in wide-eyed silence. When I finally made my way back to the front of the store, Gilles asked if I had been downstairs.

"There's more?" I asked incredulously.

"Lots more," he answered and pointed the way.

Off I went. But this was not your ordinary basement. First, you have to walk through a set of 8' x 8' steel doors, and then descend a long, domed, cavernous walkway. Think of walking into a gigantic wine cellar.

It was incredible. The ceilings going *down* to the basement were 10 feet *high*. Everything was made of dark red brick; and despite being next to a busy train yard for 100+ years, the interior looked rock solid. I ran my hands along an old conveyor belt in the middle of the walkway, left over from the days when *Merchants Distributors* owned the building.

Everything in the basement is oversized; from its unusual height, to the massive Douglas fir beams and oversized steel doors. Again, the best way to describe the basement is solid.

From the basement looking up the conveyor belt, 2007 (Photo TLS)

On a later date, I was taken on a guided tour of the rest of the building by Jody, a sales assistant, who shared my enthusiasm for its architecture. It was like being in the building that never ended. We would walk into one room, and I would think that was the end of the tour, and then we would keep walking. One of the highlights of the tour was an old pine post behind the front desk with 'Rossport' stamped on it, a poignant reminder of the days when this now sleepy village was a prosperous fishing and lumber town.

The credit for restoring this building goes to the owner of *Furniture Recycle*, Gilles Mondoux. Gilles told me that when he first purchased the building, it was in bad shape; there were massive oil stains on the floor, the bricks needed work, several doors were no longer functional, most of the light fixtures were missing and the heating system needed to be overhauled. To name a few of the problems. But he persevered through months of renovations to open up the massive 9,300 sq. foot showroom, a 2,000 sq. foot workshop and the underground labyrinth.

The massive beams in the basement, 2007 (Photo TLS)

It is clear that this is not your ordinary building. I asked Gilles if he knew anything about the building's history. He said he thought it had been used as a horse stables in the past. Now that was certainly not the response I was expecting, but it would explain the massive interior structures; the walls and beams had to withstand not only the rumbling railway, but bucking broncos as well. To find out, I did some digging in the local newspaper and the Henderson Directory. And sure enough, in 1914, 133 N. Hardisty Street, the current location of *Furniture Recycle* was owned by the *Fort William Horse Exchange*. In the days when horses were the *horse* in horsepower, the *Fort William Horse Exchange* sold and traded horses. I found two ads in the 1911 edition of the *Fort William Daily Times Journal* advertising an upcoming sale.

Encouraged by this experience, I continued to collect pieces of information about other buildings on Hardisty Street. Another Hardisty Street building that caught my eye was the Symes-Telfer Building. This three-storey, red-brick warehouse on the corner of Hardisty and Leith Street stands out a bit more that the other buildings in the area because of its arched front door and large keystone with the Symes-Telfer name engraved on it.

Symes-Telfer Building, 2007 (Photo TLS)

The warehouse was built in 1910 and named after the men who owned it: the Telfer brothers of Collingwood, Ontario—who manufactured Telfer biscuits—and William Symes of Fort William.

A check of the Henderson Directories suggests the building has pretty much always been a warehouse and distribution centre for various businesses. But in 1914, it was also rented by the 96th Lake Superior Regiment (later redesignated The Lake Superior Scottish Regiment).

I contacted Captain David Ratz, the unit historian of The Lake Superior Scottish Regiment to see if he had any information about what kinds of activities would have gone on there.

He told me the building was used as the headquarters and weapons (rifle) storage for No. 3 and 4 Companies (later renamed C and D Companies). He further explained:

> It was one of several buildings rented for this purpose over the years. This was typical of the Militia in Port Arthur and Fort William at the time since no government built armoury was available. In 1913 an armoury was built on Park Street (now Avenue), Port Arthur. However, the Fort William companies of the 96th still used rental accommodations. I am not sure if such things as social events, dances, dinners, parties, etc., were conducted in the facility. As part of the extracurricular activities of a part-time military unit these types of things were common. My impression from the newspapers is they used the local hotels for such galas. Simpson Street, one of the main commercial centres, had several such hotels.

During World War I, the 96th Regiment, or the 'Lake Sup's' as they were affectionately known, fought as part of the 52nd Battalion. They acquired a reputation for independence and bravery and went on to receive 380 decorations, including a Victoria Cross for Captain Christopher Patrick John O'Kelly for his bravery at Passchendaele in October 1917.

There are no records as to how long the 96th used the Symes-Telfer building. But even this brush with military history is pretty impressive.

Not all of Hardisty Street's history is tied up in warehouses. It was also once the location of the grand Kaministiquia Hotel located at the corner of Dease and Hardisty Streets. The four-storey Kaministiquia was built in 1891 by the Canadian Pacific Railway to meet the demands of the increased traffic to the city. The CPR's records show that the railway sold the hotel in 1906 and it was torn down a few years later.

The next article is a rather quirky story I found in the local newspaper about one of the hotel's more flamboyant guests. In 1904, the 'celebrated scientific palmist', Madame Bayla, stayed at the hotel while in the city on business. Madame Bayla boasted that she had been schooled at the *Occult College of India and France* and had read the palms of royalty and peerage. She would be in Fort William for the next 10 days to tell fortunes, for only

$1.00, and to look over some property she owned—it must be a good sign when a fortune-teller invests in your city.

The Kaministiquia Hotel, c 1900 (Thunder Bay Public Library)

Fort William Daily Times Journal, November 29, 1904

PALMISTRY RESULT OF HARD RESEARCH

Madame Bayla Explains Difference Between Palmistry and Fortune Telling

Madame Bayla, palmist. That is the modest inscription on the door of Room 15, Kaministikwia Hotel. Yesterday afternoon a representative of the *Times Journal* visited Room 15 and in response to his knock a bright faced young woman opened the door.

If any person visits the Madame and expects to see a women often pictured in song and story as one who reads the stars and palms, he will be mistaken, for

there is none of the old-time notion of the wrinkled face and walking stick about Madame Bayla.

She is a French woman, dressed in the latest modern fashion and showing in her features and speech the highest type of refinement. The reporter stated his business and remarked that he was there to interview her in regard to her scientific knowledge of palmistry—her art or profession—not knowing just what name to use.

"I will admit, to start with, Madame, that I—"

"Don't believe in it, eh?" queried Madame.

"No, not that I don't believe in the scientific principles of palmistry, but that I am ignorant on the subject."

"Most people are in the same position as yourself," said Madame. "But I am always glad to talk to any person on the subject. I have studied it for a number of years and under the most able exponents of the art.

"The science of palmistry must be disassociated with anything like fortune telling, for it is based on facts that actually exist and that have been carried through many, many years to prove their accuracy.

"The hand is the particular index of the character, of the aims and ambitions and reflects as nothing else does the elements of success or failure in a person.

"I have just come from Winnipeg, where I have been most successful."

"Do you count success by the number of clients, or do you mean that your reading of the palms has actually been of benefit to some persons?"

"Oh, I don't count success by the dollars I take in. I have been successful in the fact that men and women have benefited by what I told them. I will give you an example. Before the elections a gentleman came to my apartment and said he had placed a bet of $1,000 on Evans and asked whether he would win or lose.

"'You will lose,' I said. 'Your hand shows that you are on the eve of a heavy loss and if that is what you have done I advise you to at once place another bet on Bole.'

"He did so and saved his thousand. He gave me $3 but he should have made it $50. Success to a professional person depends on whether other persons benefit by what they advise, but not on the number of those who consult."

Madame Bayla began the study of palmistry when 18 years of age and after perfecting her studies visited the continent of Europe, perfecting herself in the language of Germany, Italy and Spain, thus being able to speak five languages fluently. She will remain in Fort William for 10 days or more.

"You see," said she. "I have more of an interest here than merely practising my profession. I own some property here, having recently purchased some while in Winnipeg. I want to look that over and decide whether to put it again on the market or hold it for great growth that I am told is sure to come to your town."

European Bakery

European Bakery, Simpson Street, 2009 (Photo EAW).

Year Built: 1910
Architect: Unknown
Style: Vernacular
Heritage Status: None

European Bakery is one of my favourite bakeries in Thunder Bay. Any bakery that has been in business for over fifty years—on Simpson Street, no less—must be doing something right. This unassuming bakery has managed to thrive when just about all of the other businesses around it have gone under.

In the summer of 2007, I asked Richard Wronowski, the owner of *European Bakery*, if I could interview him about the history of his bakery. Over the years, I had become a fan of his delicious rye breads and his famous poppy seed roll.

It turns out Richard is also a history buff and was willing to share a wealth of information about the bakery and his own family history. The only problem with our arrangement was that I would show up at 3:00 pm for our weekly interviews, only to find out that he had already sold out of bread for the day!

The bakery traces its history to 1950, when it opened as the *Canada Bakery* owned by a Ukrainian baker named Mr. Chrusz. When the bakery first opened, Simpson Street was the bustling commercial centre of downtown Fort William.

Apparently, Mr. Chursz tried out three other locations in the city for his bakery, before he settled on the Simpson Street location, which he liked because the underpass to the East End was just outside his backdoor.

I asked Richard if he knew what the building had been before it was a bakery. He said he thought he remembered his grandfather telling him it had been a billiards hall in the early days. But he wasn't sure.

Although I didn't realize it at the time, I had also, unwittingly, been doing research about the early days of *European Bakery*. Remember the Abdous? We'll come back to that.

First the Wronowski family. The Wronowski men have a long history of leaving Poland. Richard's great-great-grandfather was the first to leave, emigrating to California to try his hand in the Gold Rush of the 1850s. Next, his great-grandfather left and ended up in New Jersey. Then his grandfather Leon left, made his way to Winnipeg and then to Fort William where he was granted a homestead on Highway 61.

In 1965, Richard's father, Tadeusz, convinced Communist authorities that another generation of Wronowskis should be allowed to leave Poland. Tadeusz hadn't seen his father since 1927.

So once again, the Wronowskis packed up and left their homeland. But getting out of Poland during the Communist era was a lot harder to do than in his grandfathers' times: in fact, when they left, the five members of Richard's family were the only passengers on the flight from Warsaw to Paris, extravagantly attended to by five flight attendants.

In Poland, the Wronowskis were master bakers. Tadeusz was the manager of a big bakery in Dzialdowo, an ancient town of 24,000 in the north of the country, and Richard was his assistant. Father and son worked their bakery ovens 24-hours a day pumping out 800 2kg loaves per day.

When the family came to Canada the Wronowskis continued with their profession. Richard's father first worked at *Safeway* until he bought *Canada Bakery* in 1973 and renamed it *European Bakery*. Richard and his wife took it over in 1985.

Lucky for us, the family brought with them their recipes and skills from the old country. To this day, Richard uses the same recipes he and his father did in Poland. That means his breads are made without preservatives, enhancers, fat, sugar, or eggs. Only flour, water, a bit of salt and a homemade bread sponge go into making his ryes (light, medium and dark), sourdough and white breads, which he makes six days a week.

Two days a week he also makes a classic Polish dessert bread called makowiec (ma-KOH-viets). Makowiec is a sweet roll stuffed full of poppy seeds, the only one like it in the city.

His other specialities include raisin bread, walnut cake (which he makes at Christmas and Easter), cinnamon buns and apple sweetbuns. As if all of this wasn't enough, on Sundays after church, on their one day off, his wife, Danuta, also makes ham sausage.

Now, let's get back to Richard's building. The building at 642 Simpson Street has been put to good use over the years. As far as I could tell, it has pretty much been continuously occupied since it was built in 1910. And Grandfather Leon was right; it did used to be a billiards hall.

This is where the Abdou connection comes in.

In doing my research on the Abdous, I learned that by 1914 Charles Abdou, one of the Abdou sons, had opened up a billiards hall at 642 Simpson Street, the current location of *European Bakery*. His brother, Caeser, owned the *Economy Store* right next to it.

The billiards business must have been pretty lucrative back then. The 1914 Henderson Directory lists eight billiards and pool rooms on Simpson Street alone and a whopping 24 in Fort William.

The building remained a pool hall between 1914 and 1950, with a mouthful of name changes every few years—from the Wenger and Andrachuk pool room, to the Rech and Schaffen pool room, to the Jack Polski pool room. A reminder of Fort William's diverse ethnic makeup.

From 1950 onwards, the building has enjoyed its second life as a bakery—which undoubtedly cut down on the number of brawls and cigar smoke it had to endure.

In its various forms, Richard's building has been part of the fabric of Simpson Street for 100+ years, a considerable achievement considering our throwaway culture where many modern buildings have a lifespan of only 40 years.

Richard's bakery is an example of recycling at its best. But, of course, that's not the most important reason to admire *European Bakery,* that would be for the baking. Although be forewarned, after you have tasted Richard's fresh-baked poppy seed roll, you can never go back to store-bought. Just make sure you get there early.

Murphy Block

The Murphy Block, Simpson Street, 2007 (Photo TLS)

Year Built: 1904
Architect: Unknown
Style: Vernacular
Heritage Status: None

Of all of the buildings in this book, the Murphy Block literally forced its way in. This building was not on any of my original long or short lists. In fact, I didn't even know it existed.

One day after visiting the Thunder Bay Museum, I decided to take a walk around the neighbourhood. I was at the corner of Simpson Street and Victoria Avenue and noticed the sign: "JAS MURPHY/ WHOLESALE & RETAIL/ COAL COMPANY/ 112 SIMPSON ST" painted in white on the side of a three-storey red brick building. Coal Company? The advertisement seemed a couple of decades out of date.

Lettering on the Murphy Block, 2007 (Photo TLS)

I didn't think anymore about the building until I came across a reference to the 'Murphy Block' in a 1905 edition of the local newspaper. Where was the 'Murphy Block'? I couldn't immediately place the building until I remembered seeing the white lettering on the side of the building on Simpson Street, and I connected 'JAS MURPHY' to 'Murphy Block'.

I am glad this building was so persistent in getting my attention; it is a good reminder that history requires vigilance if we are going to care about it, and when vigilance has been lacking, it requires elbow-grease.

Local Union No.53 marching down Simpson Street, early 1900s. The Murphy Block is the second building on the right. (Collection EAW)

"What Happened Here?"

My interest in this building was piqued by a short announcement in the paper on April 7, 1905. It read:

A general meeting of the Operatic Society will be held tonight in the Murphy Block, which it is hoped all members will attend, as well as any others who are interested.

My first thought was: opera happened here?

Piecing together short announcements in subsequent editions of the paper, I learned that the Operatic Society's first performance was to be Gilbert and Sullivan's *Iolanthe* in a mere six weeks. This production would also be the inaugural performance at Fort William's beautiful new City Hall and Opera House. (Later on, I was surprised to learn that locally-produced operas and other large-scale productions had been happening in the Twin Cities since the late 1800s [Scollie 2008]).

I kept reading. Now I needed to know how the performance turned out. Straining my eyes to read the newspaper's miniscule font, I came across a review of opening night. Much to my relief, the company's 46 person ensemble (12 principals, 34 chorus) pulled off a heralded performance. Just for fun, the review is included here.

Fort William Daily Times Journal, May 31, 1905

IOLANTHE SCORED IMMENSE SUCCESS

Local Talent Showed Themselves to Great Advantage—Again Tonight

The opera Iolanthe, put on last night by local talent under the direction of Mr. W. Sheridan was a most decided success, the staging, costumes and singing being even better than was ever produced by professional companies. A chorus of 34 voices gave great volume to the whole opera and it was carried out with a vim that fairly took the audience by storm. The auditorium was filled and from start to finish the applause was constant.

It was observed, too, for the principal parts were in hands that portrayed the characters and showed the study and training they had gone through.

The plot of the opera centres around Phyliss and Strephon and these two parts were filled by Mrs. McNaughton and F.W. Holley respectively.

Mrs. McNaughton's beautiful soprano voice was never heard to better advantage. Her lines were clear and distinct and she acted the part she represented.

The cast of *Iolanthe* on the stage of Fort William's City Hall, 1905
(Thunder Bay Historical Museum Society)

Mr. Holley as Strephon shared the honours both in acting and singing. He has a clear baritone voice and the part fitted him well.

Mrs. Bole as Iolanthe, the fairy mother and wife of the Lord Chancellor was one of the best of the principals. The part required good acting and good command of oneself and Miss Bole has both requirements. Her contralto voice has a clearness that draws her hearers to her and she couples with her voice a sweet face and lovely manner.

The Lord Chancellor was Mr. A.J. Boreham. He had all the pompousness such a character requires and his dialogues and solos were sufficient to bring him well-earned praise. It is a difficult part, with more to remember than in any of the others, but Mr. Boreham was able to deliver the goods. His was the comedy part and he made the comedy.

Mrs. G.W. Reynolds was queen of the fairies and when she was selected for the part every person knew it would be well acted and well sung. She did just what her friends expected of her and brought down the house. Her singing and acting were both without a flaw and she took a most difficult part without hesitation.

Lord Mount Ararat was taken by E.R. Wayland and he surprised his most intimate friends by his characterization of the part. His solo was one of the features of the opera, his recall showing the estimation of his work. He has a really fine baritone voice.

Mr. Davis was Lord Tolloller and his singing was another feature of the opera. He has a tenor voice of good range and in chorus is a power.

The three other principal fairies were Celia, Mrs. Wayland, Leila, Mrs. E.E. Wood and Fleta, Mrs. D.W. Black. These parts are all good ones and require both singing and good acting.

But how about Prince Willis? Who would recognize the stately sentry who did not mind making love to a 'loidy' in Mr. M.S. Beeston? He looked every inch his part and for a character could not have been improved upon.

The train bearer was not so insignificant as many might suppose him to be and in contrast with the Lord Chancellor he made a decided hit. He hadn't a word to say nor a line to sing, but when it comes to kicking, Mr. Spragge had the goods.

Mrs. W. J. Rapsey as accompanist has been of great value in putting on the opera. She has been faithful to the work and she is the kind of accompanist who knows what to do and helps the singer over many a rough place.

Mr. Sheridan, the musical director, has worked hard. He must have done so. How else could he have taken 46 people, not one of whom ever took a part in such a performance, and turned them into opera singers? His was the guiding hand and any person knows what sacrifices it takes to train that number, who are doing it simply for the charity that stands behind it [the McKellar Hospital] and what personal amusement it furnishes.

The officers of the society are:

President—Peter McKellar

Vice-President—Mrs. G.A. Graham

Secretary-Treasurer—A.E. Fenton

Executive Committee—E.R. Wayland, Mrs. Deacon, Mrs. C.W. Jarvis, E.E. Wood and the officers

The Fort William Orchestra furnished the music and it came up to the standards of that excellent organization. The opera will be repeated tonight and it is hoped the people will give it the patronage it deserves.

Architectural drawing of the Murphy Block, *The Daily Times Journal*, 1904

The more research I did (read the more elbow-grease I put into it), the more times I came across the Murphy Block as the scene of other upscale social events in the early 1900s. But that shouldn't come as a surprise to us once we learn that James Murphy (1863-1928), the former Mayor of Fort William, and the building's owner and namesake, was one of the wealthiest and most respected men in town. I couldn't resist one more trip down memory lane. Below is Hester Hope's description of a 'Ladies' At Home' she attended at the Murphy Block in 1905. Consider it another lesson in peeling back the layers:

The ladies of the G.I.A. gave their first 'At Home' in their lodge room, Murphy Block, last evening and it was one of the most successful events of the season. On account of the lack of room the ladies had at first intended to entertain upon a limited scale only, but the affair grew beyond their first expectations and

there were fully 200 guests. Of all the social affairs of a like nature that have been given in the Twin Towns, the G.I.A.'s 'At Home' was the most enjoyable.

The fair hostesses vied with one another in making each guest personally welcome and happy. Cards and social chat occupied the hour and everyone was enjoying it immensely when the order to clear the floor for dancing came down the long room, and then the fun and merriment commenced and never flagged until the wee small hours. The music was perfect, indeed it could not have been bettered, and everyone was determined that his or her neighbour should thoroughly enjoy the evening.

The ladies of the G.I.A. are indeed ideal hostesses and they have demonstrated their ability to take first place in the front rank of entertainers, and I cannot praise them too highly for the hearty, spontaneous manner of their entertainment, which was so natural and graceful from each lady who wore the pink carnation (the badge of the order) and marked that the expression came from the depth of hearts anxious to give pleasure to others.

There was no cold formality about this event, no one felt outside or unwelcome. Among the ladies who did the honours with such perfect grace and tact were noticed Mrs. Marcy, Mrs. Bennett, Mrs. D. Malcolm, Mrs. Sheridan, Mrs. Armstrong, Mrs. Kelly and Mrs. Kidd.

Shortly after midnight a delicious supper was served and then dancing was again resumed until the arrival of the special car to carry away the Port Arthur guests.

Just before the 'good-nights' were said a short and impromptu program was given. J.C. Fregeau sang 'The Gallant Forty-Two.' Mr. O'Hagan gave a beautiful solo and Mr. Robinson step-danced. The whole company then joined hands and united their voices in the parting song of 'Auld Scotland' and three cheers for the G.I.A.'s.

One of the committee whispered to the writer, "we mean to have another good time shortly," and I am confident that I voice the sentiments of everyone privileged to have been present last evening when I say "May it be very soon." The G.I.A. is an organization which has thoroughly mastered the difficult art of entertaining.

Lion and gnome capitals, Murphy Block, 2007 (Photo TLS)

What about the Murphy Block today? Sadly, its facade is almost unrecognizable compared to the 1904 architectural drawing of the building on page 195. The only lingering remnants of former grandeur are five white pilasters, made of Indiana limestone, which if you look closely, will notice are capped by a delicately carved, albeit worn, lion, gnome, bird or bat (see previous page).

On a brighter note: the same James Murphy who built the Murphy Block also built the 'Murphy House' on Selkirk Street, one of the most beautiful houses in Thunder Bay.

The Murphy House on Selkirk Street, built 1912. City of Thunder Bay Heritage Property (Photo TLS 2008)

Demolition I

These things that happened years ago and that don't matter to anyone are long-gone wind and rain. Ephemeral, meaningless. But they amount to forces that shaped the rocky earth and waterways (the buildings and institutions and beliefs and histories) that made you. Guard against its theft, the past of the place that made you. At least notice it, if you cannot save it.

Melissa Holbrook Pierson, The Place You Love Is Gone

Please excuse the quality of the images on the following pages. I decided to include them because they may be the last remaining photos of these buildings. I found the images in the local history files at the Brodie Street Library; they are photocopies of articles and headlines from local newspapers.

Although, perhaps, it is appropriate that these images are blurry and of poor quality, symbolic of our fading memories.

PROGRESS DOOMS P.A. RESIDENCE

A small, restful park with an historical plaque on it is proposed for this site at 420 Arthur street, St. Patrick's Square. The city plans to widen the street here and the former Norman C. Lunan home will be demolished. The parks board will be asked to maintain this location as a park. A plaque may be erected here, marking the 1870 march of Colonel Wolsley up Arthu Street on his way to the Re River Rebellion. The Luna family occupied this residenc for more than 50 years.

—Staff Pho

Port Arthur News-Chronicle, April 27, 1965. "A small, restful park with an historical plaque on it is proposed for this site at 420 Arthur Street [Red River Road], St. Patrick's Square. The city plans to widen the road here and the former Norman C. Lunan home will be demolished. … The Lunan family occupied this residence for more than 50 years."

Old-Time Edifice To Be Razed

Pictured is an historic old Fort William edifice at 121 North May Street which is to be eliminated. The building dates back to 1887 when it was built on Simpson Street as one of the earliest schools in city history

The Daily Times-Journal, June 29, 1957. "Pictured is an historic old Fort William edifice at 121 North May Street which is to be eliminated. The building dates back to 1887 when it was built on Simpson Street as one of the earliest schools in the city history."

Landmark To Go

The 60 - year - old Vickers Residence and the Quonset Hut of McKellar General Hospital are due to be torn down in the next few days to make way for future development of the hospital. Both buildings had deteriorated in recent years to the point where they could no longer be utilized. The residence built in 1910 for resident student nurses was replaced with a modern structure some years ago. Two young girls passing by the complex are leaving after an inspection of one of the city's landmarks.

— Staff Photo

Newspaper and date unknown. "The 60-year Vickers residence and the quonset hut of McKellar General Hospital are due to be torn down in the next few days to make way for the future development of the hospital…The residence, built in 1910 for resident student nurses was replaced with a modern structure some years ago."

End Is Near For Homes Built in Early 1900s

Sailors' Institute To Be Demolished

Demolition of building eventual, no matter what

Landmark Razed. Old Police Station

Impressive Mansion Demolished To Make Room For Expressway

Pioneer Days Home To Soon Disappear

By AUNE CARELIUS

OLD CONMEE HOME ON COURT ST. RIDGE

Newspaper and date unkown. "Destined to vanish soon is the ridge-top house [Court Street] of James Conmee…a railway contractor in the early 1880s, he was the second mayor of Port Arthur…The Conmees moved into the house on the hill around 1890…Tenders have been called for the demolition of the empty mansion, the site is to be used for additional parking spaces for [St. Joseph's] hospital's users."

LANDMARK GOING

An historic north ward landmark is going down under the wrecker's hammer today. The old Pouncy's Studio located on N. Algoma St., at the top of Cameron St., is being torn down to make way for a day-care center. The English Tudor style house has long been admired by Port Arthur citizens and its passing is viewed with regret by many.

—Staff Photo

The News-Chronicle, April 12, 1972. "The old Pouncy's Studio located on N. Algoma St., at the top of Cameron St., is being torn down to make way for a day care centre."

Still I cannot but think it is an evil sign of a people
when their houses are built to last for one generation only.
There is a sanctity in a good man's house
which cannot be renewed in every tenement that rises on its ruins;
and I believe that good men would generally feel this;
and that having spent their lives happily and honourably,
they would be grieved, at the close of them,
to think that the place of their earthly abode, which had seen,
and seemed almost to sympathize in,
all their honour, their gladness, or their sufferings,--
that this, with all the record it bare of them, and all of material
things that they had loved and ruled, and set the stamp of
themselves upon—was to be swept away.

John Ruskin, 1909

UNUSUAL VIEW — A new look at the demolition of old Central school is provided in this photo by Barry Craig, taken from the roof of the May street Customs building.

Newspaper and date unknown. "A new look at the demolition of old Central School is provided in this photo by Barry Craig, taken from the roof of May Street Customs building." Central School was demolished in 1960 to make way for Paterson Park and a parking lot.

Demolition II

There was one way to have known this was coming. It was buried in the local news and letters-to-the-editor sections, which you should have been reading instead of believing the world news was somehow more important. Nothing has more impact on life than the fate of the neighbour's hydrangea.

Melissa Holbrook Pierson, The Place You Love Is Gone

Prospect Avenue School

Prospect Avenue School, c 1912 (Collection EAW)

Built: 1912
Demolished: 2002
Square Footage: 26,000 ft^2
Embodied Energy Lost: 36,140,000 MBTU
Equivalent Litres of Gasoline: 1,202,871 (Embodied Energy & Demolition Energy)

Miss Gossell's class on the front steps of Prospect Avenue School, 1915. The stone columns at the base of the portico can be seen (Thunder Bay Public Library).

Francis Street School

Francis Street School, c 1904 (Thunder Bay Public Library)

Built: 1904
Demolished: 1982
Square Footage: 37,403 ft^2
Embodied Energy Lost: 51,990,170 MBTU
Equivalent Litres of Gasoline: 1,730,425 (Embodied Energy & Demolition Energy)

Cornwall Avenue School

Cornwall Avenue School, 1941 (Thunder Bay Public Library)

Built: 1907
Demolished: 1997
Square Footage: 22,500 ft^2
Embodied Energy Lost: 31,275,000 MBTU
Equivalent Litres of Gasoline: 1,040,943 (Embodied Energy & Demolition Energy)

The vacant lot where Cornwall Avenue School used to be, 2007 (Photo TLS)

Take proper care of your monuments,
and you will not need to restore them.
A few sheets of lead put in time upon the roof,
a few dead leaves and sticks swept in time out of a water-course,
will save both roof and walls from ruin.
Watch an old building with an anxious care; guard it as best you
may, and at any cost, from every influence of dilapidation.
Count its stones as you would jewels of a crown;
set watches about it as if at the gates of a besieged city;
bind it together with iron where it loosens;
stay it with timber where it declines; do not care about the
unsightliness of the aid; better a crutch than a lost limb;
and do this tenderly, and reverently, and continually,
and many a generation will still be born and pass away beneath its
shadow. Its evil day must come at last; but let it come declaredly
and openly, and let no dishonouring and false substitute deprive it
of the funeral offices of memory.

John Ruskin, 1909

Fort William's City Hall

Fort William City Hall, Donald Street, lit up for Christmas, 1939
(City of Thunder Bay Archives)

Built: 1905
Demolished: 1966

Front entrance and gardens of City Hall, c 1910. St. Andrew's Presbyterian Church is in the background. (City of Thunder Bay Archives)

Statue in front of City Hall. Caption reads: War memorial presented by Fort William Women's Patriotic Society. Unveiled Oct 19, 1921. (Collection TLS)

The tower has been removed, c 1950s (City of Thunder Bay Archives)

Demolition, 1966. The new City Hall is in the background.
(City of Thunder Bay Archives)

Canadian Bank of Commerce

Canadian Bank of Commerce, corner of Red River Road and Cumberland St., c 1910
(Collection EAW)

Built: 1905
Demolished: 1975

A horse and sleigh passing the Canadian Bank of Commerce, c 1910. (Thunder Bay Public Library)

Demolition of the bank, 1975. (*The News-Chronicle.*)

Therefore, when we build, let us think that we build forever.
Let it not be for present delight,
nor for present use alone;
let it be such work as our descendants will thank us for,
and let us think, as we lay stone on stone,
that a time is to come when those stones will be held sacred
because our hands have touched them,
and that men will say
as they look upon the labour and wrought substance of them,
'See!—this our fathers did for us.'
For, indeed, the greatest glory of a building is not in its stones,
nor it its gold. Its glory is in its Age, and in that deep sense of
voicefulness, of stern watching, of mysterious sympathy, nay,
even of approval or condemnation,
which we feel in the walls that have long been washed
by passing waves of humanity.

John Ruskin, 1909

St. Louis Hotel

St. Louis Hotel, Victoria Avenue, 2003 (Photo TLS)

Built: 1892
Demolished: 2005

St. Louis Hotel

J. P. DOYLE
Proprietor

ROTUNDA

FORT WILLIAM

The following description accompanied this 1913 advertisement for the St. Louis Hotel:

The St. Louis Hotel is situated in the heart of Fort William's business district, and owing to the excellent manner in which the business is conducted, enjoys a splendid patronage in every department. The building is a brick-and-stone structure, the front refaced with white stone, and besides being practically fireproof is very attractive and up-to-date in appearance. The hotel is conducted on the American plan, a free bus meets all trains, and every effort is put forth to make this an attractive headquarters for the commercial trade.

The hotel has accommodation for one hundred guests. Employment is furnished to a staff of twenty-four people and patrons of the St. Louis know from experience that the service is of the best in every department.

Mr. J.P. Doyle, proprietor of the St. Louis for the past eight years, came here from Sault Ste. Marie. The excellent reputation of this popular hotel tells its own story of Mr. Doyle's ability as a hotel man.

City Livery

City Livery, Cooke Street, 2007 (Photo TLS)

Built: 1903
Demolished: 2008
Heritage Status: 'Non-Designated' Heritage Property. The Heritage Advisory Committee determined it did not warrant 'Designated' Heritage Status June, 2008. It was demolished shortly after.

THE CITY LIVERY, SALE AND BOARDING STABLE

JOSEPH GRAHAM, Proprietor.

Good Single and Double Drivers

And Up-to-Date Rigs

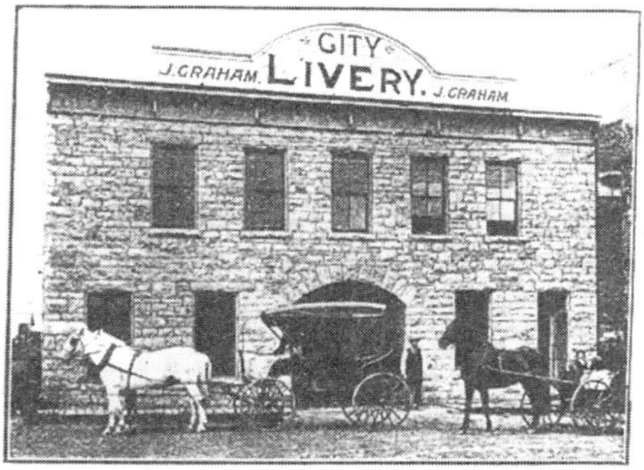

First-Class Speedy Drivers for Social Turnouts and Commercial Driving

Places of Interest in the Vicinity, and Distances by Driving

Current River Rapids and Falls	3 miles	Slate River Valley Mines	17 miles
Shuniah Mine	3 "	Dawson Road, a natural ave. for	20 "
McIntyre River, Oliver and Dawson Roads	6 "	Kakabeka Falls (120 ft. high)	22 "
Mount McKay (1000 ft. high)	7 "	Beaver Mine	25 "
McKenzie River, trout fishing	14 "	Badger Mine	26 "
Carp River, trout fishing	16 "	Silver-Mountain	38 "
Thunder Cape, (1350 ft. high)	16 "	Whitefish Lake	41 "
		Nepigon River (famous for trout)	65 "

Advertisement for the City Livery, 1915

CPR Station, Port Arthur

Canadian Pacific Railway Station, Water Street, c 1907 (Collection TLS)

Built: 1907
Demolished: 1976

Architectural drawing of the station on the front page of the *Port Arthur Daily News* Tuesday, December 18 1906.

Port Arthur Daily News, Friday, November 29 1907

OPENING OF THE NEW STATION

Is Made Occasion of Brilliant Social Function for Charitable Purpose

Fine New Building Will be Placed Into Service by the C.P.R.

The new Canadian Pacific Railway was dedicated to the cause of sweet charity last evening at its formal opening and the novelty was thoroughly enjoyed by a large number of people from the two cities.

It was a happy thought of the management to open the new depot in this pretty way and the graceful act was fully appreciated by all.

Everything was lovely in the eyes of the many guests and they admired the interior of the building and complimented the genial smiling superintendent, Mr. J. G. Taylor, upon the excellent taste displayed in the colour scheme. The ballroom proper was the general waiting room, a wide open space with a splendid floor. The dancers, as they glided in and out, also

utilized the men's waiting room, but the floor here was not as pleasing to the flying feet so the favoured spot was the larger room.

The only part of the depot furnished as yet is the ladies' waiting room, and it is a very nicely furnished room, done in green and polished oak, with mission furniture.

Charming Picture

The smart assembly of guests presented a charming picture to the onlooker. There were many very pretty gowns worn by the ladies and the buds in their white gowns added that lighter touch which goes to make up the scene of festivity that is so pleasing. Mrs. Strathy, who was the convenor of the ball, and to whom belongs much of the credit of the whole affair, is an artist in managing an event of this kind, and to her excellent ideas belongs the praise for the rosy success that crowned the evening.

The patronesses were all charmingly gowned and radiant with goodwill and happiness. This welcoming circle of ladies included Mrs. Taylor, who wore black silk; Mrs. Carrick, who was richly costumed in a white Brussels lace robe over white silk; Mrs. Ruttan, who looked very well in black net over black silk; Mrs. G. S. Clark, in pale blue silk; Mrs. Laurie, in white net over silk, and Mrs. Robarts, who was very pretty in pale blue silk. Mrs. Strathy was beautifully gowned in cream taffeta silk with trimmings of chiffon lace and motifs of rose point with touches of pink velvet.

Some Of The Gowns

Among the most attractively gowned guests were:
Mrs. McKibbon in mauve voile
Miss McFarlane in cream voile and silk
Miss Burriss, blue eolienne, lace trimmed
Miss Ferne, white muslin and lace
Mrs. G.W. Brown, brown silk
Miss Moore, white silk with touches of pink
Miss McDougall, white organdie
Miss Layburn, white silk
Mrs. J. Gordon, cream voile, trimmings of green velvet
Mrs. Hewitson, cream silk, lace trimmed
Miss Hunter, white organdie
Miss H.B. Dawson, blue silk
Miss Downing, white silk
Miss Ruttan, pale blue silk
Miss Dorothy Ruttan, pale green silk
Miss L. Demuth, embroidered linen
Miss Walsh, cream silk with lace trimmings
Miss Arnold, white silk
Miss M. Stewart, blue flowered organdie
Mrs. Fenton, blue satin
Mrs. Read, white silk
Mrs. W. Gordon, blue flowered organdie
Miss Whitney, white silk with touches of black velvet
Mrs. G. Hodder, black net over white silk
Miss Stafford, white satin
Miss Caisse, blue voile
Mrs. F. Jones, white organdie

Mrs. L. Walsh, navy blue silk
Miss Gibbs, white muslin
Miss Wink, black silk
Miss Nelson, white organdie
Miss Keefer, white muslin
Miss Roberts, white organdie, lace trimmed
Mrs. Roberts, blue striped organdie inset with lace
Miss Livingstone, champagne silk, velvet trimmed
Miss McLaughlin, white muslin
Mrs. Dennison, blue stripped muslin
Mrs. Chipman, black silk

The delightful music provided by the Gordon-Boldue orchestra added greatly to the enjoyment of the evening.

Supper was served in the baggage room at midnight and everyone enjoyed this original supper room which was very nicely decorated.

Handsome Building

The new station is a structure of particularly graceful design, built of Menominee pressed brick faced with the handsome white stone from the Tyndall quarries in Manitoba.

The most striking feature is, of course, the massive but graceful square tower rising to a height of 65 feet from the centre of the building, with provision for the installation of an enormous clock with faces on the four sides of the tower. This clock will not be put in the tower until next spring.

Demolition of the station's 65-foot tower, April 1976. (Photo by Roy Piovesana/ Thunder Bay Historical Museum Society)

Beneath the tower is the imposing main entrance, facing on Van Norman Street, and directly opposite the entrance on the track side of the building is the ticket and telegraph office, while on either side opening off the central hall are the ladies' and gentlemen's waiting rooms handsomely and modernly appointed and furnished.

The main portion of the building, including the ladies and gentlemen's waiting rooms, has a frontage of 100 feet, while shelters of graceful design, supported by brick pillars, extend on either side, that on the north a distance of 132 feet, and on the south 72 feet to where it joins the baggage and express building.

Large Floor Area

This latter has a floor area of 2,000 square feet, 1,200 of which is devoted to the baggage department and the remaining 800 feet to the uses of the Dominion Express Co.

Surrounding the whole structure is a concrete platform 380 feet in length, laid flush with the height of the rails in conformity with the new government regulation which is intended to prevent the possibility of passengers falling from a raised platform beneath the wheels of trains.

The heating plant is of steam and is located in a basement under the north portion of the main building. The floors throughout are of maple laid on sleepers set in concrete, which makes one of the finest floors in Canada and constitutes a new departure in floor construction.

Actual Opening Tonight

The actual opening of the station will take place this evening upon the arrival of the regular express No. 1 from Montreal. This train will take the track fronting immediately upon the platform of the new building and the passengers will leave on the city side instead of the lakeside as formerly. The baggage will also be handled from the new building.

Y.M.C.A.

YMCA corner of Donald and Miles Streets, c 1912 (Collection EAW)

Built: 1912
Demolished: 2009

SECTION TWO **The Daily Times-Journal.**

FORT WILLIAM, ONT., THURSDAY, APRIL 20, 1911

The Y.M.C.A. Question—What is a Boy Worth?

His Mother says he is worth all the Money in all the Banks in all the World. $100,000 BY MAY 1st

"What is a boy worth?" asked Peter McKellar and the other members of the YMCA campaign on April 25, 1911. This was the start of an unprecedented fundraising campaign in which the fine citizens of Fort William took it upon themselves to raise the unheard of sum of $100,000 by May 1—a mere seven days later. Of course, they took Sunday off to attend church.

The 150 campaigners were split into two groups—the 'Young Men's Team' and the 'Business Men's Team'—with the Young Men's Team issuing a bold challenge to the Business Men's Team: try to raise more money than us.

The goal of the campaign was to build a four-storey YMCA on the corner of Miles and Archibald—an investment in the youth of the city. As Judge McKay of Port Arthur put it:

It was better to build a house at the top of a cliff than a hospital at the bottom.

Rather than discuss the architectural details of the demolished YMCA, which would entail a description of what was its sturdy brick facade and limestone accents, the stringcourse located between the second and third floors, or the metal cornice that ran along the top of the building—or discuss the wastefulness of the demolition of this building (read the section *Embodied Energy* for my thoughts on the subject)—I have decided to include the heartwarming story of the YMCA's fundraising campaign because it speaks to the spirit of the building.

The story of the YMCA is a story about community coming together for the good of the next generation of young people.

The campaigners talked about "conserving the boys" and helping shape the "future fathers of the city". Speeches were peppered with such inspirational quotes as: "Not as little as we can, but as much as we dare"; and Peter McKellar's rallying cry: "If we are going to have a greater Fort William, we need a better Fort William".

Today the memory of that extraordinary fundraising campaign is at risk of being lost with the YMCA's demolition. But we shouldn't use that as an excuse to forget the goodwill and generosity generated by this building.

A New One Needed

Fort William Daily Times Journal, April 25, 1911.
The caption under the cartoon read: "Condition of the present YMCA quarters on Donald Street, in the old Baptist church."

DAY 1: April 25, 1911

SECTION TWO

The Daily Times-Journal.

TEN PAGES

IT ISN'T A QUESTION OF CAN OR CAN'T—
"IT'S A QUESTION OF WILL OR WON'T

I BELIEVE FORT WILLIAM'S GOING TO DO IT—
NOTHING IS IMPOSSIBLE IN FORT WILLIAM

One Hundred Thousand Dollars—This Thing I Do This Week

Y.M.C.A. CONTRIBUTIONS THIS AFTERNOON TOTAL $28,841

More Than Quarter of Amount Required
for Y.M.C.A. Subscribed
Contributions During First Few Hours of Big Campaign
Exceed Most Sanguine Expectations
McKellars Give $5,000

"What are our boys worth?" is the slogan of the week.

The keynote of last night's meeting in the Maybee store was –"Look after the boys."

About 150 earnest men, drawn from every section of the community, partook of a cold collation as the initial move of a week's strenuous life, for strenuous is the life indeed of those who seek to obtain funds from the public purse for semi-public purposes....

Catchy Mottos

The room in the Murphy Block [see p. 188] last night was full of business. There were good business faces, a good business tone in the speeches, and a good business manner in which things were hustled through last night. On the walls were the messages:

"Not as little as we can, but as much as we dare." "Victories that are easy are cheap." "Everyman something everyday," and other cheering battle calls....

Conserve The Boys

Judge McKay of Port Arthur then described the benefits to be derived by the young men and the businessmen, and how the older businessmen had become enthusiastic over the Y.M.C.A. in Port Arthur. To the boys it was equally beneficial, or it was better, to build a house at the top of a cliff than a hospital at the bottom.

They talked about conserving their resources, and the boys were the most difficult they had to conserve. They had to train them, and they lost their investment unless they made good men of them. There was one way to help the boy, and that was by the establishment of such institutions as the Y.M.C.A. To the mothers it meant much, for however great the achievements of Canada's public men, the work of the mothers was greater still.

"A Jolly Good Fellow"

Peter McKellar on rising was greeted with, "He's a Jolly Good Fellow," followed by cheers. He said he had come to the conclusion that their efforts would be successful, though he had thought that they were a little too soon in starting owing to the unsettled state of the country, but now he was convinced that the city needed the building, and they must have it. Their churches were well established, and it was now for them to help the Y.M.C.A. No city would expect to do much without such an association in their midst...

It was a fact that if they were going to have a greater Fort William they would have to have a better Fort William.

Employers of labour should remember that character had to do with dividends, and the better the men, the better the work. They must stick to their work; they must cooperate and sink all their differences, and give the purpose of the campaign right of way that week.

Just before the gathering closed with the benediction, E.R. Gavin challenged the Business Men's committee through a hugh poster on the wall which was let down by Dr. Withrow and which read as follows:

The Gauntlet

"The captain and members of the Young Men's committee throw down the gauntlet to the Business Men's committee to raise more money during the campaign than the latter—and see more people. Signed W.L. Bird, H. Martin, P.J. Lake, A. McIssac, Dr. Boyd, E.E. Boon, G.H. Adair, G.R. Evans, Alf. Cooper, D. Kerr, R.H. Neeland, E.R. Gavin."

E.S. Rutledge rose from his seat, and his simple, "I accept it", was greeted with cheers, and one of the most enthusiastic meetings ever held in Fort William came to a conclusion.

DAY 2: April 26, 1911

The Daily Times-Journal.

FORT WILLIAM, ONT., WEDNESDAY, APRIL 26, 1911.

Lord Strathcona, High Commissioner for Canada, Believes in the Greater Fort William

He has Backed it up to the Tune of $10,000.—How Much do You Believe?

On Day 2, the newspaper introduced the 'YMCA Clock' to keep track of the running total. The clock's hand would move around its face as donations came in. And the donations kept pouring in: in one day, the Young Men's Team raised $2,970 and the Business Men's Team $4,760.

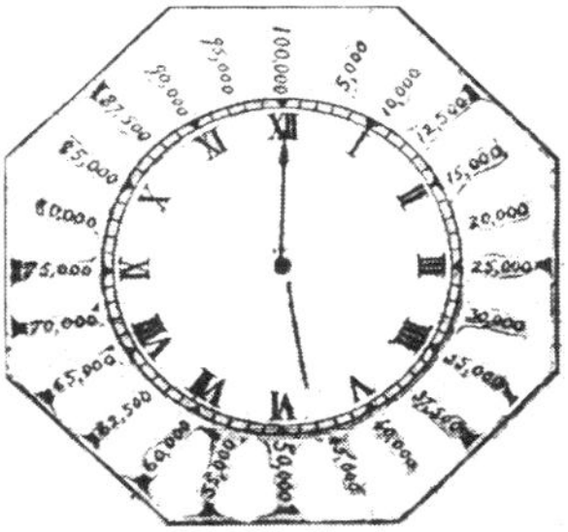

YMCA Clock

But the biggest surprise of the day was a $10,000 donation from Lord Strathcona cablegramed from London, England. Lord Strathcona, one of the founders of the Canadian Pacific Railway, had made several visits to the city and had many friends here.

Although there was a drop in donations from Day 1, that was to be expected, and spirits were still high.

"Hank it all," L.R. Clarke, one of the campaigners was quoted as saying in the local newspaper. "I can't give any time to business while this stunt's on."

Amount raised so far: $46,571.

DAY 3: April 27, 1911

The Daily Times-Journal.

TWENTY-SIXTH YEAR SECTION ONE FORT WILLIAM, ONT., THURSDAY, APRIL [illegible] TEN PAGES

Y. M. C. A. Contributions This Afternoon Total $57,327

On Day 3 $10,756 was raised to bring the grand total up to $57,327. An impressive figure, but that wasn't good enough: the headlines of the day urged people to open up their wallets even more:

"There is a Tide in the Affairs of Men, which, Taken at the Flood, Leads on to Fortune."

"Neglected! –Neglected! –Neglected! –Fort William Knows no Such Word. $100,000 Will Establish a Big Line of Credit With the World."

See Them Boost it

DAY 4: April 28, 1911

The Daily Times-Journal.
FORT WILLIAM, ONT., FRIDAY, APRIL 28, 1911.
'WHAT WE HAVE WE'LL HOLD." The Slogan of the Bull Dog on the Flag.
"WHAT WE AIN'T GOT WE'LL GET." The Slogan of Fort William on the Kam.
To Get the Minute Hand up to the 100,000 Mark Needs Some Reaching and Digging--Just Two Days More.

Fort William Daily Times Journal, April, 28, 1911

EVERY HOUR SEES Y.M.C.A. WORKERS NEARER HUNDRED THOUSAND MARK

Teams Cheer When Announcement of Another Successful Day is Made at Noon Luncheon
Many Good Prospects Will be Visited During Final Days of Big Race

Eight thousand eight hundred and thirty-nine dollars for the past 24 hours to noon was the result of subscriptions to the number of 190, and though there was a dropping off to the tune of nearly 2,000 the result was good.

For practically three days working, the sum of $66,166 stands to the credit of the friends of the Y.M.C.A. and everyone is confident that the $34,000 necessary to make good will be secured before the campaign closes on Monday night next.

Today the Young Men's team was in great spirits. They cheered just for the joy of it, until through pure contagion the staid, sober, sensible businessmen got up and howled too. It is not too much to say that there is not a single worker in a single team that possesses

the slightest doubt that he and his co-helpers will be unable to put the movable finger of the clock onto the $100,000 mark.

There are still a large number of citizens of good standing to canvas, and it is a pleasing sign to note that several men who have already subscribed have forwarded further help as they have become more convinced of the worthiness of the cause—helping the future fathers of the city.

"Aim high there is a whole lot of room at the top," so says Sayer and his continual exhortations to get busy is the greatest factor in the campaign....

As Mr. Sayer said, there can be no standing still now. Appealing to a railway man present at the luncheon he asked if an engine slipped when on a grade what it was that they did. The answer came, "Sand", and in response to the question what would happen if they didn't sand when the engine hung up came the single word, "Stall".

It was either sand or stall, continued Mr. Sayer, and they simply had to pull the campaign through. Cries of confident jubilation answered him, after which Messrs. Murphy and Maybee were loudly applauded on the motion of the speaker thanking them for the use of the store during the week.

DAY 5: April 29, 1911

The Daily Times-Journal.

TWENTY SIXTH YEAR SECTION ONE FORT WILLIAM, ONT., SATURDAY, APRIL 29, 1911 TWENTY PAGES

Y. M. C. A. Contributions This Afternoon Total $74,947

To the Citizens of Fort William,
One hundred of our busiest are giving their time and money to make possible the new Y.M.C.A. in our City. There is a great deal yet to do. It is impossible to see every person, we therefore make this appeal to all to assist us in any and every way possible. No amount is too small; none can be too large. Let every person do his best and our success is assured. Remember we have just one day more; our aim is $100,000 by May 1st. Do it now.

Yours very sincerely,
W.J. Hamilton, Pres. Y.M.C.A

April 29/1911

DAY 6: NO CAMPAIGNING ON SUNDAY, APRIL 30

DAY 7: May 1, 1911

SECTION TWO. The Daily Times-Journal.

The Y. M. C. A. Crew are Bending, Every Man to his Oar The Boat's Nose Swiftly Approaches the Goal The Last Second Tells the Tale.

If you Haven't Helped a Little Do it Now.

Fort William Daily Times Journal, May 1, 1911

MAKING FINAL SPURT FOR THAT BIG STAKE

The witching hour of the night approaches when pockets yawn and tightwads cough up their plunks. There is a tide in the affairs of the Y.M.C.A. tonight which taken at the flood leads on to $100,000. The collectors are crying with no voice in the wilderness: "Give us the limit, or give us death."

Weary, footsore, but as lively as a week ago, the captains have hurried and harassed their teams till the mere thought of a rest is treason. With a ferociousness and pertinacity worthy of a Jesse James, has the noble and gallant band of workers held up the citizens until the clock face bears something sinister in its expression to every person with a banking account. And the conclusions they have come to—that is, the common garden citizen—is that for their credit's sake they must pay, pay, pay....

Certain it is that nothing has aroused the enthusiasm of Fort Williamites as a body in the past, as this well-

organized and determined effort to raise a sum of money that was thought to be beyond the possibilities of the city, and never before, have so many different personalities and opinions been brought together to work in such perfect harmony as on the present situation. The work now is a triumph in itself, and should that steadily progressing hand reach its stationary confrere, then indeed, can the collectors be greeted with: "Well done, thou good and faithful servants."

On May 2, President Hamilton announced they had done it! $100,000 in seven days. A great cheer went up when the tally was read at a banquet at the Murphy Block.

Six months later (November, 1911), the YMCA's cornerstone was laid, which included a time capsule containing: the Bible (King James version); Annual Report of the Board of Trade for 1910; Financial Statement of the City for 1910; The Daily Times-Journal; The Morning Herald; Associated Men; 'the coins of the realm'; and 'postage stamps of the Dominion of Canada'.

A year after the cornerstone was laid, the YMCA was opened.

YMCA cornerstone. Inscription reads "Spirit, Mind, Body"
(Photo Dawn Kannegiesser-Mitchell 2009)

Mariaggi Hotel

Mariaggi Hotel, Water Street, c 1905 (Collection TLS)

Built: 1884
Demolished: 1988

The Mariaggi Hotel is a good reminder of the ebb and flow of Thunder Bay's history. At one time, it was one of the grandest hotels in the country, and in its later years, a lowly rooming house until it was ultimately demolished in 1988. If we aren't careful its stories will vanish with it. The Mariaggi has always seemed less of a building to me, and more like the backdrop for a theatrical performance, complete with dramatic scene changes and colourful characters.

Act I

The Mariaggi started out as the Northern Hotel in 1884. With its sweeping views of the waterfront and luxurious accommodation, it was elegant enough to host the likes of royalty and heads of state, including the Prince of Wales (who later became King George VIII, before abdicating), as well as Canadian Prime Ministers Sir John A. MacDonald and Sir Wilfred Laurier.

In the late 1800s and early 1900s, the Northern hosted some of the Lakehead's most prestigious social and political events. One of the most important of which was the ceremonial driving home of the 'Last Spike' in 1901 on completion of the CNR's Winnipeg-Port Arthur rail route. Guests of the ceremony were brought by special train to a site near Slate River. Railway buffs will be interested to know that this 'Last Spike' was forged with silver from the Porcupine Mine in Gilles Township. It was engraved on four sides with the following words:

1. Canadian Northern Railway
2. Port Arthur-Winnipeg Section
3. Driven on Completion
4. December 30th, 1901

After the outdoor ceremonies, the guests returned by train to Port Arthur for dinner at the Northern Hotel. *The Fort William Daily Times Journal* (Dec 31, 1901) captured the festivities:

Shortly after 8 o'clock the guests began to assemble at the Northern Hotel and with the arrival of the guests of the evening a bonfire was started on the shore of the bay and a torchlight procession made a fitting getting to the day's proceedings.

The dining room of the Northern was indeed one of the attractions of the whole long day. Two long tables ran along the length of the room , crossed at the lower end by another where sat Mayor Matthews and the invited guests...

The decorations were simply magnificent; Union Jacks were hung in festoons from one end of the room to the other, and the side walls and ceilings were a mass of flags and bunting.

On the lower end wall was a banner bearing the firm name, "Mackenzie, Mann & Co." and the motto, "Energy, Enterprise, Ability." On the right hand side of the wall was another large motto, "Port Arthur to Liverpool, 4,000 miles"; and on the opposite wall, "Port Arthur! The Silver Gateway to the Golden West."

Around the tables was a miniature railway track with trains of cars and a telegraph line, making up the story of the completion of the track.

The meal served that night was fitting of the occasion:

Blue Points on Half Shell
Consomme
Sherry
Lake Superior Whitefish and Tartar Sauce
Braised Fillet of Beef
Fried Potatoes with Mushrooms
Champagne

Roast Partridge with Bacon
Roast Wild Duck with Jelly
Roman Punch

Baked Cream Potatoes
Chicken Salad
Claret

Deep Apple Pie with Devonshire Cream
Wine Jelly
Charlotte Russe
Ice Cream
Celery and Cheese
Nuts and Raisins
Fruit
Café Noir

The hotel's reputation was further enhanced when the charismatic Frank Mariaggi (1847-1918) bought the hotel in 1904. Mariaggi, who was born in Corsica, Italy, made his way to Winnipeg in the 1870s—where he made a name for himself as a chef and hotelier, opening his first hotel, the namesake Mariaggi Hotel (which incidently, is still in operation). After he bought the Northern Hotel in Port Arthur, he immediately renamed the hotel after himself, and announced he would spend $10,000 to refurbish it.

One of his top priorities was to recreate the 'grotto' bar he had opened at his Winnipeg hotel. The grotto bar was a dark, cave-like cocktail bar, its walls covered with green-coloured stucco leaves. Perhaps feeling homesick, Mariaggi designed the bar to resemble the forest caves he was fond of in his native Corsica. Further changes to the hotel were detailed in a newspaper article in the *Fort William Daily Times-Journal* on November 23, 1904:

GREAT CHANGES IN THE NORTHERN

Frank Mariaggi, the new proprietor of the Northern Hotel, accompanied by J.J. Carrick, arrived from Winnipeg last evening and at once got busy laying out plans for the remodelling of the house on a thoroughly modern basis.

When seen by the reporter this morning, Mr. Mariaggi was busy engaged going over the house from cellar to garret, making mental notes of required improvements and he briefly outlined them.

In the first place, the bar will be moved to the southwest corner of the house, where the kitchen is now situated. It will be a faithful reproduction of the bar in the Mariaggi's in Winnipeg, the interior being done in stucco finish.

Next to the bar and occupying part of the present dining room will be a day and night café, thoroughly up-to-date in every particular.

The rest of the dining room will be fitted up as a billiards room. The dining room will be moved to the north side of the house where the billiards room and bar are located, and the kitchen and pantry will be in the northwest corner now occupied by the laundry.

Upstairs on the first floor elaborate changes will be made. Nearly all of the rooms on that floor will be refurnished and remodelled to make them equal to anything in the country.

A number of rooms will have bathrooms attached and telephones, as well as other modern conveniences.

The third floor will also be thoroughly overhauled and brought up to the standard of the rest of the house.

Mr. Mariaggi is a hustler, as is evidenced by the fact that he proposes to have all these improvements completed by January 1, when he intends to open the house under the name of "The Mariaggi", the same as his Winnipeg house.

Before he left Winnipeg he engaged men to do the stucco work on the bar and be ready to come at a moment's notice.

The 'grotto' bar, c 1920. Manager, and later owner, Max Hurtig is standing at the end of the bar. (Collection TLS)

Just a couple of months after its remodel, the Mariaggi was the scene of a glittering *Bal Poudre* or Powder Ball (a ball fashioned after Louis XVI and Marie Antoinette's royal court) hosted by the Ladies' Aid of the General Hospital. This ball was to be a proper *Bal Poudre* and strict dress rules were announced in the *Fort William Daily Times Journal* on February 18, 1905:

Those desiring to attend the calico and poudre ball on March 3 at the Mariaggi Hotel, Port Arthur, can obtain tickets from the Bazaar or at Crooks' drug store.

This will be a real calico ball: no one will be allowed to wear silk or satin; but muslins, organdies, voiles, crepes, chiffons and laces will be correct. Everyone will undoubtedly powder their hair, although this will be left to individual taste. Flour is said to be the best agent to use, and it is said that powdered hair makes the homeliest face pretty and attractive.

If I could insert myself into one story in this book, it would be this one. I like to imagine I am one of the 300 guests who attended this beautiful ball. As per the dress code, I have powdered my hair and chosen a gown of Nile green muslin. Not to be outdone by the younger set, some of the older society women wore rubies and diamonds.

The night starts with a 'Grand March' in which all of the guests gather in the hotel's drawing room and then descend the grand staircase into the ballroom. What a magnificent sight the parade of powdered wigs and fancy gowns must have been!

Unfortunately, I couldn't find a photo of the evening, but the following newspaper article gives us just enough information to let our imaginations run wild.

Fort William Daily Times Journal, March 4, 1905

THE BAL POUDRE BRILLIANT SUCCESS

The Bal Poudre given by the Ladies' Aid of the new General Hospital in the Mariaggi Hotel, Port Arthur, last evening was one of the most brilliant society events of this and many other seasons.

The big hotel had been given over unreservedly to the ladies by Mr. Mariaggi and the committee in charge had made the most of the opportunity offered, and the result redounded to their credit.

At nine o'clock the large drawing room and reception hall were crowded with those intending to enter the Grand March. The march was led by the President of the Ladies' Aid, Mrs. J.L. Meikle and Mrs. F.S. Wiley, followed by the President of the McKellar Hospital Aid, Fort William, Mrs. C.W. Jarvis and Mr. R.M. Hamilton.

About three hundred joined in the Grand March, and as they came down the wide stairway, through the hall into the ballroom, they made up a scene for the spectators that will not be forgotten, one that has never been equalled in either town.

The ladies with their powdered hair and jewels, their light, bright coloured gowns; the gentlemen wearing coloured lapels and cuffs and powdered hair (in many cases, ye olde tyme peruke was seen) presented a brilliant moving picture that delighted the eyes of the beauty lover.

As the dancers entered the ballroom they openly expressed their surprise and admiration at the beauty of the setting which clever hands had prepared for the picture in which they were to be a living part.

The large room had been transformed into a fairyland of beauty. Never before in the history of Port Arthur has there been such handsome decorations worn.

Flags and bunting had been used with a most lavish hand, and perfect taste had guided the arrangement. Bright red and white completely covered the walls, with Union Jacks and Dominion flags everywhere in evidence as drapery.

At one end of the room, placed in the centre, was the photo of the new hospital, surrounded by flags of all sizes. Mr. Mariaggi and Mr. Lytle were the chief decorators, and the result demonstrated their artistic abilities and splendid taste.

The floor was perfect for dancing and the program as given by the Guerard orchestra all that one could desire.

At midnight supper was served in the dining room. The ladies had all observed the rules laid down by the committee in charge and were correctly gowned for a Bal Poudre.

It would be impossible to describe, with the space at command, all the many pretty gowns noticed; the prettiest however, were worn by the following ladies:

Mrs. J.L. Meikle looked very sweet in a mauve muslin with touches of black, and beautifully dressed coifffure, poudre and diamonds.

Mrs. C.W. Jarvis was charming in pale green crepe cloth, with black velvet bands, poudre coiffure.

Mrs. Neil McDougall looked well in nile green muslin, poudre and pearls.

Mrs. McKibbin was handsome in cream voile lace, and poudre.

Mrs. F. Jones was gowned in the style of 1830, large blue flowers upon a cream muslin, a girdle of soft blue silk, with brilliants and poudre.

Mrs. W. Gordon was very pretty in another picture of that past time when fair dames looked so dainty and sweet.

Mrs. Gordon wore a large flowered pink muslin, hair powdered and dressed low with pink roses.

Mrs. C.W. McLean was very handsome in a pink mull, poudre and roses.

Mrs. Gibbs wore white embroidered mull over pink.

Miss Powley was gowned in pale blue and poudre.

Miss Clark, white organdie and lace.

Miss Burk wore white organdie and poudre.

Miss E. Vigars, pale blue mull, roses and poudre.

Miss Dobie, white organide and poudre.

Mrs. Nelson wore pink muslin with white lace, and poudre.

Mrs. Shera looked very nice in champagne and black.

Miss Robinson wore while muslin dotted with black, and poudre.

Mrs. J. Munro, blue and fawn linen, brilliants and poudre.

Miss Meikle was sweet and charming in pale green and pearls.

Mrs. Chipman wore mauve and black lace, poudre and brilliants.

Mrs. E. Hunt, white organdie, pink silk girdle, and carnations.

Miss Jackson, lavender muslin, poudre and roses.

Miss McFarlane, white organdie with lace, and roses and poudre.

Miss Keefer, white muslin, poudre.

Mrs. Hunter, blue organdie, and lace.

Miss Mills, pink muslin, poudre and rubies.

Mrs. Shields, pale blue muslin, poudre, and pink roses.

Mrs. Dawson, linen, poudre, and pink carnations.

Miss Downing looked very pretty in white book muslin, poudre and pink roses.

Mrs. A. Ross, white over green, poudre and diamonds.

Miss Bishop, white persian lamb, poudre and roses.

Mrs. Bennett, white organdie and lace, poudre and rubies.

Mrs. P. Whalen, white mull, roses.

Miss Ritchie, white muslin and lace, poudre and carnations.

Miss Davidson, white organdie over pink roses and poudre.

Miss Bruce, white muslin.

Miss Bonin, white muslin, lace and poudre.

Miss M. Johnston, white organdie with touches of green, poudre and red roses.

Miss Bakewell (Winnipeg), pink mull, roses.

Miss Daniels, red organdie, poudre.

Mrs. Mahoney, black net, poudre and diamonds.

Miss Wooley, white lustre, poudre and carnations.

Mrs. Montgomery, black and white foulard, poudre, and garnets.

Mrs. Downing, black net.

Mrs. Grey, pale yellow crepe, lace trimmed, poudre and roses.

Mrs. Carrick, pink and white organdie, roses and poudre.

Mrs. Wideman, blue and brown linen, poudre and brilliants.

Mrs. A.E. Vigrars, champagne voile, lace trimmed, roses and poudre.

Mrs. R. Dobie, black net, poudre and roses.

Mrs. A.G. Vigars, white lace, poudre and carnations.

Mrs. C. Vigars, white organdie, poudre and roses.

Mrs. Friday, white book muslin over blue, poudre and roses.

Miss E. Powley, pink flowered muslin over white, poudre and garnets.

There were a number of guests from Fort William, among them were:

Mrs. Tremayne, looking very nice in white organdie and lace, red roses and poudre.

Mrs. E.A. Morton, in linen-coloured muslin, brilliants and poudre.

Mrs. Stevenson, in pink flowered muslin, poudre and roses.

Miss Brown, in pink mull, poudre and roses.

Miss Parker, champagne voile and red roses.

Miss O'Conner, white voile dotted with green, poudre and carnations.

Mrs. Morris, violet foulard and white chiffon, poudre, and violet ribbons, and many others.

The committee in charge of this ball deserves the greatest praise for the completeness of the arrangements and to Mrs. Neil McDougall and Mrs. McKibbin belongs great credit for the success of the event.

Those on the the reception committee were Mrs. Harstone and Mrs. Meikle; Messrs. Wiley, Nelson, Andrew, Lytle, Meikle, Bennett, Ray, Wideman, Shera and McKibbon. The floor arrangers were Messrs. Costigan and Dawson.

Everyone seemed to enter into the full enjoyment of the hour, and all united in declaring that of all the balls ever given in Port Arthur, this first one of the General Hospital Ladies' Aid has been the most successful in every way, and the most enjoyable.

NOTES

Mr. Mariaggi had certainly won the hearts of the ladies of Port Arthur. He simply devoted himself to their interests, and entered with a zest and vim that enthused all the workers into the work of preparation. The entire hotel was given over to the ladies that evening, and hereafter Mr. Mariaggi's name will be always held in the greatest honour and gratitude by Port Arthur's fair ones.

Bachelors' dinner at the Mariaggi Hotel in Winnipeg. Frank Mariaggi is seated at the head of the table, December 1905. (Archives of Manitoba)

Poudre, poudre and diamond dust everywhere. Mrs. A.H. McDougall and Mrs. McLean did a rashing, flourishing business in the make-up line, and they deserve much credit for their work which was perfection itself. All day Friday these ladies gave their services and materials to the benefit of the hospital.

The music was splendid, and dancing was a pleasure. The Guerard orchestra cannot be praised too highly for the program.

Act II

Despite his substantial investment and involvement in the hotel, Mariaggi didn't actually own it for very long. A year after buying the hotel, Mariaggi sold it and moved back to Corsica where he became Mayor of his hometown. In 1908, the Bronfman family purchased the hotel, thus starting another intriguing era in the hotel's history.

Like Mariaggi, the Bronfmans made significant improvements to the hotel, but kept the famous grotto bar. In 1920, *The Daily News* outlined the $23,000 in renovations the Bronfmans were making to the hotel:

From basement to top floor every room has been re-papered, floors have been re-carpeted, electrical fixtures replaced with modern lighting systems, bathrooms made modern and sanitary. In fact everything possible has been done to make the hotel homelike and cheerful.

The Mariaggi is situated on Water Street at the corner of Park. Its front overlooks the broad expanse of Thunder Bay and from all its front rooms a splendid view of the harbour can be obtained.

The old unsightly verandahs have been removed.

The main entrance is of white tile flooring covering the whole of the rotunda, billiard room and soft drink bar.

The walls are painted—for sanitary purposes—in warm brownish tones with stenciled borders. The rotunda contains two open fireplaces and is furnished with deep comfortable chairs upholstered in genuine leather.

The Rotunda, c 1920. As described in *The Daily News* (1920): "The rotunda contains two open fireplaces and is furnished with deep comfortable chairs upholstered in genuine leather." (Collection TLS)

The hotel contains 110 guest rooms capable of accommodating 165 persons. The owners intend adding twenty more rooms this winter in the space formerly used for sample rooms. These rooms will be supplied with hot and cold water and will be up to date in every particular.

The new plans also call for the construction of a passenger elevator.

The dining room is large and well-lighted and has a reputation of unequalled service. The room will seat upwards of two hundred guests at a sitting...

The Mariaggi is equipped with an up to date billiard room, containing English billiard and American pool tables; a barber shop and a bar which is one of the few of its kind in the Dominion. The bar has been a source of much comment by visitors to the hotel. It is

constructed of concrete to resemble a grotto. It was the idea of the late Mr. Frank Mariaggi, at one time the proprietor of the Mariaggi here and the Mariaggi at Winnipeg.

What makes the Bronfman era so interesting is that the family owned the hotel *and* a liquor distilling company at the height of Prohibition.

During Prohibition, the sale of intoxicating beverages for consumption in public establishments was forbidden (the government allowed the sale of alcohol for some purposes, such as scientific or medicinal). In Ontario, Prohibition started in 1916 and officially lasted until 1927, when it was repealed following an election and liquor was permitted to be sold by the Liquor Control Board of Ontario (LCBO). Prohibition in the United States, which lasted from 1920 to 1933, was even stricter than in Canada, as all manufacture and transportation of beer, wine and spirits was illegal.

Interestingly, liquor produced in Canada could be legally exported to the United States; thus began the very profitable era of rum running.

In 1924, the Bronfman family founded the Distillers Corporation Limited in Montreal (Quebec had repealed Prohibition in 1919) and later added the Seagram and Sons Company in 1928. The merger created the world's largest distilling firm.

There is plenty of speculation that during Prohibition, the Bronfmans used the Mariaggi Hotel as a liquor smuggling point to transport alcohol into the United States.

Most intriguing is a supposed rum running tunnel that was discovered in the 1970s under the hotel. In his book *A History of Thunder Bay*, Joseph M. Mauro mentions a tunnel that City crews stumbled upon while doing road work in 1978. The tunnel apparently ran from the basement of the Mariaggi down to the waterfront. The former manager of the hotel, Bud Heidrick, was apparently able to re-open the tunnel and found a pipe and pully system that ran along the length of the tunnel. In 1984, Bud Heidrick showed newspaper columnist Howard Reid where construction crews supposedly found the tunnel. Oldtimers interviewed by Mauro told him the tunnels were used to smuggle liquor onto the ships and trains that loaded in front of the hotel.

Seeming to corroborate this story, Mauro also mentions that former freight and grain handlers told him that thousands of cases of liquor were shipped from Thunder Bay to Detroit and Chicago, hidden under mounds of grain.

However, other people connected to the Mariaggi Hotel dispute the tunnel story. Clair Hurtig, the wife of Max Hurtig, who managed the hotel during the Bronfman era and then later bought the hotel from the Bronfmans and owned it until the 1960s said: "There was no tunnel, but if people want to believe it why not? It's a good story." (*Chronicle Journal*, July 4, 1984)

And Terry Hurtig, Max's grandson, flatly denied the tunnel story. He told me that the 'tunnel' was actually a natural bedrock cave under the Mariaggi that Max allowed bears to overwinter in. Max was a nature lover who kept the bears in the basement until they were older, and then brought them to his Pigeon River Lodge (for pictures of Max and the bears at the Mariaggi Hotel see Peotto, 2008).

Either way, bears or rum, it's a pretty fascinating story.

Act III

In Act III, the Mariaggi Hotel, now called the Marina Inn, has fallen on hard times. It has mainly become a rooming house for men who were displaced during the 'urban renewal' project on South Cumberland Street.

A few relics of its more elegant past remained, for instance, the two solid brass antique Otis elevators with Greek leaf motifs still ran between the floors. And the 10-foot-tall stained glass windows depicting the scene 'Morning, Noon and Night' were in place between the first and second floors until 1988.

But most of its glamour was gone. A *Globe and Mail* reporter who visited the hotel in 1982 recorded the new house rules:

> No noise after 12:00 or move out and I mean NOW—not tomorrow.
> If you give our night staff a hastle (sic) you will be moved out.
> Anyone touching fire doors will be moved out and fast—right now.
> All rents payable in advance. No pay, no stay!
> No garbage out the window.
> In case of fire alarm ring, make sure all doors closed and get the hell out.
> No wandering around halls and knockings on door. Watch your guests.

With the change in clientele, there was no need to maintain the hotel's high standards, as evidenced in the sad decline of the drawing room over the decades:

Act I: In the early 1900s, the drawing room was good enough for royalty and Prime Ministers. Here is one of the earliest descriptions of the drawing room, published in 1887: "On gaining the first floor you turn to the right into the main drawing room and parlour, 45 x 25, with entrances to the verandah. A fine marble mantle with an open English fireplace gives it an air of comfort." In 1904, remember, the drawing room was the staging area for the Grand March of the *Bal Poudre.* Imagine the powdered men and women of Lakehead society putting the final touches on their evening dresses before parading down the grand staircase.

Act II: In 1920, the drawing room was still a respectable place to admire the view of Lake Superior. The following description of the drawing room appeared in the local newspaper: "The drawing room of the hotel is one of its finest features. It is covered with a rich pile carpet and is furnished with antiques, said to be almost priceless. The chairs, setees, and tables are of solid mahogany and worthy a place in any Englishman's home."

Act III: Now compare the above descriptions with the gloomy state of the drawing room in the hotel's final days. In 1988, a journalist for the *Chronicle Journal* (August 27, 1988) toured the hotel weeks before it was demolished: "One sitting room overlooks the harbour and was probably something special in its day. The wallpaper is torn, floors are warped, an electric candelabra no longer works. Next door, a drawing room has big sliding doors that a gentleman may have pulled shut when entertaining a lady friend years ago. The room is now dark and has an acrid smell." Clearly, I was a couple of decades too late.

Long gone as well is the grotto bar and its fancy drinks and green leaf stucco walls, by the end it is just a bar, apparently famous because it only served beer, no wine or liquor. A sign posted in the bar in the 1980s read:

> To save you time and money, please be advised that music in this room for dancing Friday and Saturday night is Western with a beat, boogie and honky tonk, blues and old-time rock and roll. No disco, punk or hard rock. Thank you.

Demolition—Out of Sight, Out of Mind

In 1988, the 103-year-old hotel was torn down to make way for the Ontario Government Building on Water Street. Arguably, a more architectually pleasing building considering the final state of the Mariaggi.

Although I miss the Mariaggi's presence, I understand that times change. We can't preserve everything that was ever built in Thunder Bay, but we should be more respectful of what is already here. We can do a better job of reusing historic buildings and not letting them slide into neglect so that they 'have' to be demolished (in other words, 'demolition-by-neglect').

Not just bricks and mortar, Thunder Bay's buildings are the anchors for our stories and memories. I was thrilled to find out we once had hotels grand enough to host a *Bal Poudre*; a hockey team that played for the Stanley Cup; and to read about a time when the East End was home to twenty-five businesses. If we continue to lose our historic buildings, it will be harder and harder to keep these stories as part of our psyche. Remember Simone Weil's words: a healthy society requires its citizens to feel rooted, to be connected to their surroundings.

It is up to us to decide what kind of city we want to live in. Shouldn't we find a better way to honour and celebrate what *is* here, so that past and future stories are not forgotten?

Unseen Places of Thunder Bay

I have pinched the title of the last section of the book from Jeffrey Mehagan's website www.thunderbayunseen.com. I came across Jeffrey's site when I was doing random Google searches trying to gleam any bit of information I could for the book. When I came across his site, I was amazed at all of the work he had put into it, and I knew I had to contact him.

Jeffrey is a self-motivated local historian who is devoted to the preservation of Thunder Bay's history. He put the website together, which has hundreds of pictures and just as many stories and descriptions, on his own time, with his own funds.

What I like about his website is that he goes off the beaten track. This isn't the type of history that you will find in a textbook or a museum. Jeffrey has walked down overgrown paths and knocked on strangers' doors to find out some of Thunder Bay's most interesting history; the kinds of things you would want to know about your neighbour's old house or the odd lamp post on your street.

Whereas the theme of this book could be that there is history under just about every brick in the city, Jeffrey's website takes it one step further. There could be history under that cement slab or grassy patch you are standing on.

Considering our shared interests, I asked Jeffrey if he would write a section for this book about his favourite 'Unseen Places' in Thunder Bay. I was delighted when he obliged. His list is below.

I also thought his list would be a good way to end the book; on a positive note about just how much accessible and interesting history is out there—and how a couple of knowledgeable jaunts around the neighbourhood, armed with a few of these forgotten stories, can do the soul good.

Unseen Places of Thunder Bay by Jeffrey Mehagan

When people find out about my website and what I write about, inevitably one of the first things I am asked is: "what is the wall in the bushes in the East End?" This question completely sums up the purpose of my website: to provide answers about the history of this city to the people who live here; to tell people about the places that define this city; and to share stories that might otherwise be forgotten. Here are some of my favourite unseen places in Thunder Bay:

St. John Street Park

This little patch of undeveloped land lays across the street from St. Joseph's Hospital on Algoma Street. Originally this area was a small residential street, never paved, with a few houses. The street itself ran right overtop of exposed Canadian Shield rock. At some point, after 1920, the street was closed to traffic and the houses were removed. There were four houses on St. John Street at one point, and some of the markings of the house lots can still be seen, if one knows where to look. A little easier to find is the stump of a telephone pole for the lines that ran along the street. The lot is now being transformed into a neighbourhood park with newly planted trees and gardens and a sign proclaiming its name, no longer forgotten by development.

Hardisty Street

Running alongside the Canadian Pacific rail yard opposite the East End, Hardisty Street is a reminder of this city's heyday in the age of rail. The street is marked by current and former rail crossings throughout its entire length. It is lined by warehouse buildings, most of which have boxcar loading bays. It is easy to walk down this street, drinking in the atmosphere and imagining sixty years ago when it would have been alive with workers loading and unloading the cars, the steam of the engines in the yard, and, just across the yard, ships docked at the grain elevators and wharfs that used to line the Kaministiqua River. Each of the buildings along Hardisty has a story to tell – whether it be a fur storage building, goods warehouse or a manufacturing operation. This street was once the commercial heartbeat of Fort William and it still breathes history today.

Corner of McKellar and Miles

This simple street corner has one of the greatest pieces of forgotten Thunder Bay history in my opinion. No, I am not talking about Fort William Gardens (although it is pretty historic and classic in its design) or the giant curling stone that stands as a local landmark in front of it. Instead I am referring to the southwest corner where there stands a red brick house. On the corner of the house are two street signs proclaiming the corner of John Street and Myles Street. I couldn't tell you when they were first put there, but I can tell you that John Street was renamed McKellar in 1974 after the amalgamation of the two cities. I have no idea when the spelling of Miles was officially changed. The house has been re-painted since the signs were first erected, but the owners have been careful not to paint over the signs.

Mouth of the Current River

This area was once a prized location in the town of Port Arthur. The mouth of the Current River was a must see location for anyone visiting the Lakehead. Now, it is virtually forgotten. At the turn of the 20th century, this little slice of land was once home to various industries including a stamp mill and pulp mill. In the 1910s, the Current River Fish Hatchery was built to provide Whitefish fry for the local commercial fishing industry. The hatchery closed in the late 1960s, but the buildings remained on the site until the early 1970s. There were also bridges across the mouth of the estuary until around the same time–look closely and you might see their remains on the islands in the mouth of the river. Today this area is home to the last of the city's commercial fishing fleet. This is also a great place to see some of the lake's largest ships as they load at the nearby elevator or undergo maintenance at the neighbouring shipyard.

Freedom Park

Lying between Water Street and the railway tracks at the base of the Marina Park Overpass you will find Freedom Park which commemorates various immigrant communities and families that have come to Thunder Bay in order to escape political or military strife in their homelands. The park is a testament to the multicultural nature of our community. Each of the park's benches is dedicated to a different family. Before this land was created into a park, it was part of the CP's P Yard (which once provided rail access to the Brewer's Retail building on Camelot Street [which was formerly Cameron Street]). The current entrance to the Overpass was once the location of Graham Street, a small residential street that hugged the rails and the lakeshore before Marina Park was constructed and before the connection between Water Street and Cumberland was built. There is a cluster of trees and shrubs that once marked the front yard of the last remaining house on this scrap of street.

Carrick Street Dog Park

This land sat vacant for years before the city repurposed it into an off-leash dog park, the first one in Thunder Bay. In the land's previous life, however, this was the site of the switching yard for CN Rail's Iron Ore Trestle. Just about every single reminder of the site's previous use has been removed, save for the odd fire hydrant or light pole. What cannot be removed is the decades' worth of iron ore dust that was shaken off the pellets and the cars as they were shunted through the yard. Even though the cars travelled over one hundred kilometres from Atikokan's Steep Rock Mine to empty into the holds of a Great Lakes freighter, there was still more dust to shake loose in the yards. The ground here will be stained rust red for decades to come, a unique reminder of the industrial heritage of this city.

Little Vickers Street

This stretch of duplicated street lies between Northern Avenue and Weigand Street, just before the Neebing River. It seems very out of place as the duplication of the street does not carry on once you cross the river, nor does one stretch of street carry northbound traffic while the other carries southbound traffic. Traffic flows in both directions on either street with a small median between them. This bizarre stretch of street is one of the last tangible reminders of the Port Arthur, Duluth, and Western Railway. It was just north of here where the P.A.D. & W.'s line left the main rail line to travel on a loop through Fort William (south on Vickers and then west along Arthur). When the tracks were removed, the land was reserved as a roadway instead of sold to nearby developers. The Fort William Station was located at the corner of Vickers Street and Victoria Avenue.

McVicar Manor

This bed and breakfast on the city's north side, adjacent to McVicar's Creek, has a unique visual reminder of this city's intensely strong organized labour movements. The B&B is housed in a beautiful red stone home originally built in 1906. Much of the home's original features and building materials have been retained through the ensuing century, but for the veranda located on the south side of the building, facing McVicar's creek. The veranda seems oddly modern for such a historic home, and considering such attention to detail. But there is a good reason for the remodel: the original veranda was replaced in the 1960s after a bomb explosion! The then-owner of the house was a manager of a trucking company and, during a labour dispute, a bomb delivered to the house blew off the veranda's skirting. No one was killed in the explosion, but it did demonstrate the deep conflicts between the classes in the Lakehead at that time.

Wiley Mansion

This beautiful stone home was built in 1910 for Franklin S. Wiley, on one of the highest points in the city of Port Arthur. The house sat at the front of a huge estate. To receive an invitation to a ball at the Wiley mansion probably marked your place in the city's social scene. However, within 20 years of its construction, the mansion ceased to be a family home and was converted into apartments. Soon afterwards it was purchased by the Sisters of St. Joseph and has served as the order's home, providing care for those in the community. The estate's lands were broken up and are now home to seniors' housing, a church, and a community centre. Even though the land has been extensively re-landscaped it is still possible to trace some of the original features, such as the carriage path from Arthur Street (Red River Road) to the rear of the house where the stables would have been located.

Wiley Mansion, c 1910. The mansion's grey limestone was quarried from a mine in the Dorion-Pass Lake area (Thunder Bay Public Library)

École secondaire catholique de la Vèrendrye

The lot that this new high school sits upon is home to two excellent examples of unseen history. In the northeast corner of the lot is a large and lumpy hill with some exposed rocks. These are the remains of the Singleton Silver Mine–one of the first mines in Port Arthur. Prospect Street is supposedly named for this mine since it provided the new town with the prospect of riches. The second piece of unseen history lies along the bus loading area off Tupper Street. The large pieces of stone that border the loading area are all that remain of the stone pillars and buttresses of the former Prospect Street Public School, which formerly sat upon this site before it was closed and torn down. Apparently, the final destination of the globe that sat atop the entrance of the school is in someone's garden, although that is a rumour I cannot confirm.

And to satisfy the curiousity of those who wonder about the answer to that first question:

East End Wall

The wall is all that remains of the CPR Coal Docks coal storage, a reminder of the economic heyday of the Kaministiqua River.

Index

Additional Research References

p.5: A typical building built in the mid-20th century required the equivalent of 5 to 15 gallons of gas per square foot: These figures are from the article, 'Sustainability by the Numbers' published in *Preservation Nation*, the online journal for the National Trust for Historic Preservation. The full link to the article is: http://www.preservationnation.org/issues/sustainability/sustainability-numbers.html. (Date accessed February 2009)

p.6: Sustainable development: As defined by Powter and Ross (2005): "Sustainable development is now generally understood as requiring the presence of several "pillars" to support it—environmental, economic and social…Applying this broader definition of sustainability, the reuse and operation of existing buildings not only avoids or minimizes negative impacts on the environment through the conservation and efficient use of resources but also recognizes the role that building construction and the buildings themselves play in fostering regional and local culture and traditions; supporting community life and the economy; and contributing to the texture and humanity of the built environment." (p. 5)

p.6: When writing this book, I thought of each building as its own character: I don't want to weigh this book down with jargon, but this approach is called a phenomenological approach. Phenomenology seeks to explain or uncover phenomena though "a descriptive, qualitative discovery of things in their own terms" (Manzo, 2003: 48). The idea is to let the phenomenon, in this case the building, 'speak' for itself and guide my research.

p. 13: Captain Scott's letter: The original letter is held in the Perth Museum. The source for this letter is Joseph M. Mauro's book, *A History of Thunder Bay* (p. 49).

p. 13: Colonel Wolseley's camp, Prince Arthur's Landing, 1870: The full title of this watercolour is 'Red River Expedition, Colonel Wolseley's Camp, Prince Arthur's Landing on Lake Superior (Ontario)'. It was painted by William Armstrong in 1870. The source for this picture is Library and Archives Canada, Acc. No. 1969-3-1.

p. 14: A letter from Hugh John MacDonald: The source for this letter is: Arthur, E. (1973) *The Thunder Bay District 1821-1892: a collection of documents.* Ontario Series. No. 9. Toronto: Champlain Society: 115-116.

p. 27: On June 9, 1916, 1,385 boys of the 94th New Ontario Battalion: Information for this section was retrieved from the websites www.52ndbattalion.com and www.94thbattalioncef.ca.

p. 44: City of Thunder Bay Designated and Non-Designated Heritage Properties. List and Definitions at:
http://www.thunderbay.ca/Living/Culture_and_Heritage/heritage_properties/Heritage_Registry.htm (Date accessed August 2009)
Designated Heritage Property: "Formal designation by City By-law provides the property with protection against demolition or alteration."
Non-Designated Heritage Property: "Properties that appear on the Heritage Registry which have not undergone formal designation are provided with interim protection. The Heritage Advisory Committee and City Council have recognized these sites to be of historical interest. Owners of these properties are required to give City Council sixty (60) days notice of their intention to demolish. This allows time for Council to decide whether to begin the designation process, which provides properties with permanent protection."

p. 45: The story goes, that in 1908, the Mayor of Port Arthur: The story was recounted to Lon Patterson by J.J. Carrick and published in *Fort William Daily Times Journal*, April 1, 1962.

p. 45: Roughly the equivalent of $9,000,000 today: This figure was generated by the Bank of Canada's online inflation calculator. The calculator only goes back to 1914, so I used 1914 (instead of 1911) to do the calculation.

p. 127: Jackson quote from: Curtis, W. 2008. A cautionary tale. *Preservation.* http://www.preservationnation.org/magazine/2008/january-february/cautionary-tale.html (Date accessed February 2009)

p. 141: The eight remaining storeys of the Royal Edward Hotel: Calculated by Bob Mills of the Thunder Bay Non-Profit Housing Corportation.

Bibliography

Anonymous. 1915. Atlantic terra cotta in Canada. *Atlantic Terra Cotta.* II (4)

Arthur, E. (1973) *The Thunder Bay District 1821-1892: a collection of documents.* Ontario Series. No. 9. Toronto: Champlain Society

Basso, K.H. 2004. *Wisdom Sits in Places.* Albuquerque: University of New Mexico Press

Black, M.J.B. 1934. Fort William, Ontario Public Library. *Library Journal.* 59: 510-511

Casey, E. 1987. *Remembering.* Bloomington: Indiana University Press

Cresswell, T. and Hoskins, G. 2008. Place, persistence, and practice: evaluating historical significance at Angel Island, San Francisco, and Maxwell Street, Chicago. *Annals of the Association of American Geographers.* 98(2): 392-413

Curtis, W. 2008. A cautionary tale. *Preservation.* Retrieved from: *http://www.preservationnation.org/magazine/2008/january-february/cautionary-tale.html* (Date accessed February 2009)

Ford, L.R. 1974. Historic preservation and the sense of place. *Growth and Change.* 5(2): 33-37

Giedion, S. 1962. *The Eternal Present.* New York: Pantheon

Gunnell, A. (1993). This magnificent pile: architectural embellishments of older school buildings in Thunder Bay. Thunder Bay Historical Museum Society, *Papers and Records.* XXI: 35-60

Hayden D. 1995. *The Power of Place.* Cambridge: MIT Press

Local Architectural Conservation Advisory Committee. 1977. *Experience '77: An Evaluation of Thunder Bay Historical Bulidings.* Unpublished Document.

Lowenthal, D. 2006. *The Past is a Foreign Country.* Cambridge: Cambridge University Press

Manzo, L.C. 2003. Beyond house and haven: toward a revisioning of emotional relationships with places. *Journal of Environmental Psychology.* 23: 47-61

Maslow, A.H. and Mintz, N.L. 1956. Effects of esthetic surroundings: I. Initial short-term effects of three esthetic conditions upon perceiving 'energy' and 'well-being' in faces. *Journal of Psychology.* 41: 247-254

Mauro, J. M. 1981. *A History of Thunder Bay.* Thunder Bay: City of Thunder Bay

Mintz, N.L. 1956. Effects of esthetic surroundings: II. Prolonged and repeated experience in a 'beautiful' and an 'ugly room'. *Journal of Psychology.* 41: 459-466

Nairn, I. 1965. *The American Landscape.* New York: Random House

Oldenburg, R. 1999. *The Great Good Place.* New York: Marlowe and Company

Peotto, T. 2008. Prohibition at the Lakehead, 1916 to 1927. Thunder Bay Historical Museum Society, *Papers and Records. XXXVI*: 68-88

Pierson, M.H. 2006. *The Place You Love Is Gone.* New York: W.W. Norton

Powter, A. and Ross, S. 2005. Integrating environmental and cultural sustainability for heritage properties. *APT Bulletin: Journal of Preservation Technology.* 36: 5-11

Relph, E.C. 1976. *Place And Placelessness.* London: Pion

Ruskin, J. 1909. *The Seven Lamps of Architecture.* London: Cassell

Rypkema, D. 2007. Sustainability, smart growth and historic preservation. *Historic Districts Council Annual Conference in New York City.* March, 2007. Retrieved from: *http://www.preservation.org/rypkema.htm* (Date accessed March 2009)

Scollie, B. 2008. Theatre and music on Ontario's frontier, 1876-1907: town hall entertainment in Victorian Thunder Bay. Thunder Bay Historical Museum Society, *Papers and Records.* XXXVI: 24-52

Sovik, E.A. 1973. *Architecture for Worship.* Minneapolis: Augsburg Publishing House

Veenhof, B. (2006). The internet: is it changing the way Canadians spend their time? *Statistics Canada: Science, Innovation and Electronic Information Division.* http://www.statcan.gc.ca/pub/56f0004m/56f0004m2006013-eng.pdf (Date accessed Sept 2008)

Tuan, Y.F. 1977. *Space and Place: The Perspectives of Experience.* Minnesota: University of Minnesota Press

Vervoort, P. 1977. Meaning in old buildings. Thunder Bay Historical Museum Society, *Papers and Records.* V: 1-11

Vervoort, P. 1989. Thunder Bay's first high-rise and its terra-cotta symbolism. *SSAC Bulletin SEAC.* 14 (3): 75-83

Vervoort, P. 1998. Thunder Bay: once a city of train stations. Thunder Bay Historical Museum Society, *Papers and Records.* XXVI: 46-63

Visser, M. 2000. *The Geometry of Love.* Toronto: HarperCollins.

Weil, S. 1955. *The Need For Roots.* Boston: Beacon Press

Websites
www.52ndbattalion.com

www.94thbattalioncef.ca

www.AndersonvilleStudy.com

www.thunderbayunseen.com

http://www.collectionscanada.gc.ca/databases/census-1901/index-e.html

http://www.collectionscanada.gc.ca/databases/census-1911/index-e.html

www.thegreenestbuilding.org

http://www.thunderbay.ca/Living/Culture_and_Heritage/heritage_properties.htm

A Note From The Author

I realize that many historic buildings are missing from this book. I hope to rectify that in the future—in possible subsequent editions of the book or perhaps another volume.

If you know of any forgotten stories about Thunder Bay's historic buildings or have any old photographs that you would like to share, and possibly have included in a future book project, please contact me.

My email address is: tlsaj@riverrocks.ca

Or you can contact me by post at:

River Rocks Publishing
#331-1100 Memorial Avenue
Thunder Bay, ON
P7B 4A3